Classic Bus Tests

Edited by Peter Waller

IAN ALLAN
Publishing

Contents

Original authors as noted; all other contributions were originally uncredited.

Title page: **Typical of the Bristol K6B/ECW combination of the late 1940s is this Crosville example, No MB282.** *Crosville*

Front cover: **A 1948 Daimler CVD6 with Metalcraft coach bodywork, in Smith's Eagle Coachways livery.** *David Reed*

Rear cover, top: **A 1951 AEC Regent III with Roe bodywork, restored in Doncaster livery.** *Philip Lamb*

Rear cover, bottom: **A 1949 Daimler CVD6 with Weymann bus bodywork in Exeter livery.** *Philip Lamb*

First published 1997

ISBN 0 7110 2524 X

Code: 9707/B

Published by Ian Allan Publishing

an imprint of Ian Allan Ltd, Terminal House, Station Approach, Shepperton, Surrey TW17 8AS.
Printed by Ian Allan Printing Ltd at its works at Coombelands in Runneymede, England.

Introduction

It is amazing to look back and see what lengths the transport trade magazines went to in the 1930s, 1940s and 1950s to test new bus and coach models. It took a certain dedication to embark on a lengthy road test on a bare chassis, which was sometimes what was supplied by the manufacturers, and you get the impression that the road testers of half-a-century ago were a hardy breed.

Today buses and coaches are still road-tested by the trade press, and if it seems that today's tests are less thorough, they are probably much more realistic. As several manufacturers have found to their cost, no amount of pre-production testing in temperature extremes and on test-tracks can equal the problems that readily become evident after a few days in passenger service at the mercy of a heavy-footed driver or a heavy-handed mechanic. So today's bus tests are often in-service tests using production vehicles made available by an operator, and not specially prepared by a manufacturer. If there are problems, operators soon make you aware of them.

This splendid collection of tests from the pages of *Modern Transport* and *Passenger Transport* provides a fascinating picture of some well-loved and less common vehicle types through the eyes and the prose of the time. Many of us fondly remember these buses in daily use, while other readers may only know the preserved examples they see at rallies and museums.

The value of these tests as a historic record is further helped by the fine selection of photos, some actually taken on the tests described.

If the selection of vehicles seems unusual, this is because it reflects the tests that were available in print. As a Leyland fan I was disappointed to see only the Comet — not a *real* Leyland to many of us, anyway — was the only representative, and it seems that Leyland, either through confidence in its product, or sheer Lancashire cussedness, didn't feel it necessary to make its models available for test, an attitude that continued well into the 1970s. So there are no Tigers or Titans in this book, but the coverage of AECs, Bristols and Daimlers makes up for this, and in addition to the models that were familiar throughout Britain there are some fascinating oddities, such as the Morris Commercial, the Rowe Hillmaster, the Beadle Canterbury and the rear-engined 1957 Seddon. And the pioneering work of Midland Red on underfloor-engined designs is recognised in the test of a BMMO S9 in 1949, before the mainstream manufacturers had introduced their first underfloor chassis.

Road tests have always fascinated me, as a reader and now as a tester when we carry out our occasional head-to-head tests of historic buses for *Classic Bus* magazine. You may not agree that the buses covered in this book necessarily deserve to be described as 'classic', but the tests themselves certainly are.

Gavin Booth
Editor, *Classic Bus* magazine

Right: **The double-deck version of the AEC Q chassis was uncommon, with only some 20 being built. Bradford Corporation No 393 was the only Q-type to be operated in the city; it was new in August 1933 and was fitted with a Metropolitan-Cammell 60-seat body. It was withdrawn in September 1939 and sold the following year. It was subsequently to see service, inter alia, with Burwell & District. Bradford Corporation was also to operate the unique Q-type trolleybus (No 633).**
All photographs from the Ian Allan Library unless otherwise stated

Left: This Burlingham-bodied Daimler CVD6 was in service with Mid-Wales Motors when photographed in Cardiff's Central bus station when on the express service from Newtown.
R. H. G. Simpson

Below: This view of Hull Corporation No 172, an AEC Regent O661 fitted with Gardner 5LW engine and Massey 56-seat body, was taken in the early months of World War 2 outside the Electricity Buildings in Ferensway. Visible behind the bus are sandbags, whilst the Hull legend has been doctored on the negative as has the indicator board. Other evidence of the war — such as the white painted mudguards — has yet to make an appearance. The body of this bus was lifted in about 1950 and transferred to a Guy chassis.

Vehicle Road Tests
—(*Passenger Transport Journal* 10 May 1946)—

For some while now it has been the intention of the *Passenger Transport Journal* to carry out independent road tests of public service vehicles. Letters we have received recently indicate that there is a general desire for these tests, which, by being based on similar conditions as far as possible, provide good comparative checks of vehicles' possibilities.

To this end, we have evolved two standard procedures, one for vehicles operating under short stage town conditions and the other for single-deck coaches on long distance work with intermittent stages, so that the vehicles will be checked under genuine operating conditions. Each vehicle will carry a full test load and will already have covered a mileage of from 100-500 miles so that it is reasonably well 'run in' and will therefore give ordinary standard results. To give readers an idea of the scope of the test, the following gives the checks our Technical Editor intends to make.

Below: **A map showing the convoluted route undertaken by the various vehicles tested on the innocuous sounding *Modern Transport* Southern Test Route.**

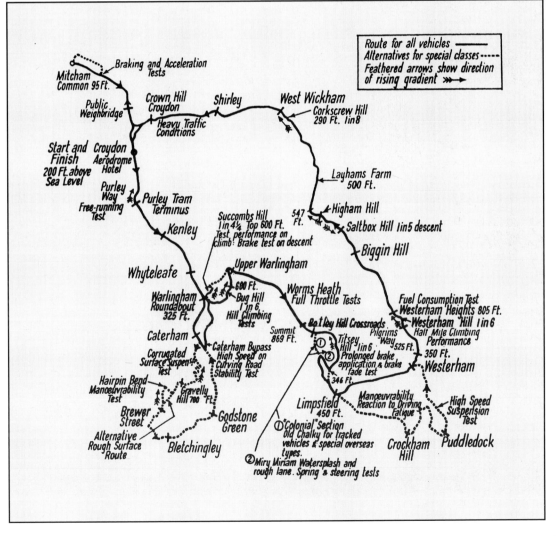

Left: **Climatic conditions could often affect the results of a test and a number were carried out during winter months. It is doubtful, however, whether a test ever faced such adverse weather conditions as this Western National AEC Regal pictured on the Minehead-Lynmouth route in early 1935.**

Below: **Many of the tests recorded in the pages of both *Passenger Transport* and *Modern Transport* described models that were either prototypes or destined to be built in relatively small numbers. The Dennis Pelican test described in July 1956 featured the unique lightweight example built that year. The vehicle incorporated a horizontal version of the five-litre Dennis engine and was fitted with a 44-seat Duple body. The chassis was eventually scrapped in the early 1970s when the body was transferred to an AEC Reliance chassis.**

Route — This will be chosen to suit the type of vehicle, and will probably cover some 60-70 miles; a route with a representative proportion of flat country and hills will be chosen. Short stage vehicles will have start and stop tests in towns.

Weather — This will be noted and allowance made where necessary if road conditions unduly affect the results.

Test load — The vehicle will carry a test load up to the legal limit.

Fuel consumption — This will be noted by a two-way run over a route with one gallon of fuel in the flow meter tank, and from this a figure for pay load ton miles/gallon will be obtained. Short stage buses will receive an additional test under town conditions with four 10sec stops per mile. (This will probably be undertaken with half a gallon of fuel.)

Average speed — This will fall within legal limits.

Acceleration — This will be checked in two ways, first by timing to give a rough and ready reading; the personal element enters so largely into stop-watch readings, however, that a second series of tests will be taken using the well-known Tapley Performance Meter. In each case the tests will be made on level roads.

Pulling power and hill climbing — These will be checked by means of the Tapley Performance Meter, readings being taken at the point of change into the next gear.

Braking — A macadam road will be the scene of these tests, and the Tapley Brake Meter will provide the figures. Checks will be made from 20mph and 30mph for the hand and footbrakes independently and then both brakes together.

Tractive resistance — This will be checked on a level road by means of the Tapley Performance Meter. The vehicle will be declutched when running at 20mph, allowed to run freely, and a reading taken to make sure that there is no undue transmission friction, binding brakes, etc. This will be the first test made.

The Tapley meters already referred to are produced by Tapley & Co of Southampton, and operate on a magnetic pendulum principle. The pendulum is carried in a bath of oil, and its movement, which is compensated for temperature variations, is transferred to the revolving indicating scale by means of a light armature and geared segment and pinion. In 1939 a report on the equipment was made by the National Physical Laboratory, who carried out exhaustive tests on specially designed runways and subsequently issued a certificate of efficiency.

We think the tests we have indicated, together with the accurate instruments available, and the co-operation of manufacturers, will provide an honest story of a vehicle's possibilities which will be of benefit to manufacturers and operators alike. We should welcome any suggestions readers care to make, however, and will incorporate them if at all possible.

Road Testing Passenger Vehicles

Editor's Note
The text for the road tests have been derived from contemporary reports in the trade press. The comments made were correct at that stage but will obviously have been overtaken by subsequent events. The dates quoted in the contents are those dates that the articles were published whilst the dates recorded in the text are those of the actual test itself. All appeared in *Modern Transport* with the exception of the following which appeared in *Passenger Transport*: Foden single-decker; Daimler CD650; BMMO S9; Leyland Comet; AEC Regent III; Morris-Commercial; Bedford/Duple Service Bus; Rowe Hillmaster'; Bedford Super Vega; Beadle Canterbury; Albion Aberdonian; and Seddon 18.

It requires only a little reflection to appreciate the enormous advance that has been made during the past few years in the evolution of the present-day heavy passenger vehicle, and it is no exaggeration to say that few other branches of engineering science have gone forward so rapidly. The buses and coaches of today possess refinements that are not even equalled by a great number of private cars; in fact, it can be contended that the British heavy commercial vehicle now leads the world in automobile design and efficiency.

This progress, however, though rapid, has not been easy, and it reflects the greatest credit on the designers, research engineers and mechanics who have contributed to the production of these excellent machines, particularly as the regulations laid down by the authorities — the Construction & Use Regulations — covering overall length and width, minimum ground clearance, axle loadings, brake layout, etc, are somewhat hampering. Added to the latter consideration there is the very strenuous work these vehicles are required to perform. The average car owner thinks he has done well if he completes 25,000 miles annually, whereas the modern bus or coach may do this in a matter of three months and, furthermore, has to carry it out on an exacting scheduled timetable.

The daily work of buses in the busy cities and towns, consisting as it does of stopping and restarting every few hundred yards, with continual gear changing and brake operation and great variations of engine speed and loads, must be one of the severest tests to which any piece of mechanism is ever subjected. To ensure, then, that a public service vehicle is quite satisfactory for normal service conditions, exacting tests and trials are undertaken both by the manufacturers and by independent observers. These tests are normally much more severe than anything that a vehicle is likely to encounter in actual service.

First of all, when a new component is designed it is subjected to tests of all types for efficiency and durability. For the postwar Leyland Titan buses, for example, a synchromesh gearbox was designed, to aid drivers in making smooth and easy gear changes without effort. To prove its reliability in service would have taken years, so a robot gear-changing device, controlled by radio valves, was set up so that thousands of changes were effected every working day. After a million or so changes the designers knew a lot more about the characteristics of everything that the new gearbox contained. Leyland engineers are not easily satisfied, however, and the first postwar Titan, the PD1, used an older type of box, the synchromesh gearbox not appearing until the PD2 chassis, with larger engine, was ready.

When the chassis as a whole has been designed a prototype is usually built and again this is tested, sometimes to destruction. One of the new Leyland passenger chassis was run from the company's works in Lancashire to Gretna in Scotland, 102 miles away, and back, three times a day, making 612 miles daily and calling for three shifts of test drivers and observers, so as quickly to get experience of the new vehicle's behaviour on the road. During such runs, which in this case totalled 41,000 miles, all run at as near the legal speed limit of 30mph for buses as possible, various tests can be carried out at will and an accurate record of fuel and lubricating oil consumption is, of course, made. Among similar test courses that of Guy motors from Wolverhampton to Llangollen in North Wales may be mentioned; this is sometimes varied by working over a Wolverhampton Corporation motorbus or trolleybus route. The Motor Industry Research Association has a test course for similar purposes near Nuneaton.

On top of all this, each individual production chassis is tested by the majority of manufacturers after construction and before delivery to the customer. Indeed, the majority of heavy vehicle builders are naturally most exhaustive in their road testing of a newly assembled chassis and, with the exception of about three firms producing lighter and cheaper models on a mass-production scale, put each one through a gruelling series of tests over a course from 60 to 100 miles in length. During this time a thorough check is made of every chassis component and the fuel consumption and power output must be to a definite standard. Above all the chassis must be dimensionally correct and pass the very rigid Ministry of Transport examination for a certificate of fitness.

On the other hand those road tests conducted by individuals outside a factory organisation, such as

experts of the technical press or representatives of road transport undertakings, are primarily to obtain by their own methods the best performance that can be produced.

As an example of the factory road test, let us examine the procedure at the Southall plant, where AEC vehicles are built. Here, the factors governing all test procedures are calculated with meticulous care in the Research & Experimental Department. Commencing with the engine power curve, the technicians compile the theoretical performance of every chassis type under every conceivable condition, so that when the finished product arrives at the test shop, the staff has little else to do than see that each chassis behaves in a conventional manner. Now, having described the basic requirements of an AEC test, we can examine the details of the organisation to see how they are fulfilled in practice.

When passed from the assembly line, one member of the test staff is responsible for formally accepting each chassis. Certain preliminaries are then applied by the chassis testers before a road convoy is assembled. For instance, the level of the water in the radiator is examined, and checks are taken of the oil levels in the engine, gearbox and rear axle, as well as in the brake equipment where necessary. All tyres are carefully scrutinised for possible damage and their pressures are corrected. All these items must be entered on the test card before the chassis is moved from the shop. Next, each tester must ensure that the load is secured safely to the chassis and that trade licence plates and driving mirror are fixed properly.

All particulars having been entered on the card, the testers set off on one of nine selected routes. Upon leaving the works the chassis are not permitted to exceed certain prescribed speeds for the first 20 miles: 20mph for passenger models and 15mph for goods-carrying types. After covering that distance any stiffness should have worn off, leaving a run of 80 miles in which observation of general behaviour and performance can be made. A stop is made after 10

miles to check the chassis for possible overheating of the transmission or wheel bearings; at the same time each chassis is inspected for water or oil leakages. No authorisation is given to the testers, however, to undertake major repairs or adjustments. If this becomes necessary the chassis returns to the works for rectification, then testing starts afresh.

The test run then continues with observation of hill-climbing performance, the results obtained being entered on the test card, together with comments on engine noise, vibration, etc. Should there be any doubt about the engine power during the climb it is repeated, but no interference is permitted on the road with the fuel injection pump timing. This is to overcome any artificial impression of engine performance caused by fixing the timing, as the fuel pumps used on AEC chassis are accurately bench tested, and no improved performance is possible from subsequent alterations. Later in the test run, each convoy is halted, when each chassis is checked over by the test foreman and driver. On this occasion minor adjustments and a general tightening up is permissible. A main stop in a long run is used as the occasion for a general review of the behaviour of each chassis in the convoy, when the foreman investigates any deficiency in performance reported by the testers.

On the return journey all the brakes are tested for efficiency after a prolonged application and for brake drum squeal. The brakes are finally tested, however, on arriving back at the works. Fuel observations include measurement of the fuel and oil consumption during the test; if not to the prescribed standard, this means that the chassis is not fit for the second or fuel consumption test of 10 miles. Any chassis that is non-standard is required to undergo a stop and restart on the factory test-hill. On completion all cards are filled in by the testers, scrutinised by the Superintendent of Sales Inspection and filed away for reference for a period of six months.

The independent testing of private motor cars by technical or trade journals commenced soon after World War 1 and in 1927 the first test of a commercial vehicle by an automobile engineering expert, unconnected with the manufacturer, was undertaken. Prior to the inauguration of these tests by

Right: **Pictured in December 1934, this was the latest Bristol/Gardner single-deck chassis on test. Note the additional weights added to the chassis to simulate the presence of both a body and a full load of passengers. Also visible is the seat behind the driver that was occupied by the test observer.**

the weekly newspaper *Modern Transport*, it was considered by those who were pioneering the scheme that besides being of an exhaustive nature the tests should be carried out over a standard route, thereby enabling readers of the journal to be confident that the report was the result of a thorough investigation and the opportunity for a comparison between makes and types. There is, of course, another obvious reason for selecting a standard route; this is the attainment by the tester of a sound knowledge of the route, thus obtaining the optimum performance from the chassis.

In the search for a really good route, all the conditions that were likely to be encountered in actual service were required with a few additional hazards of a colonial nature. The route selected must provide for acceleration, braking and fuel consumption data, for observation of general running; for a selection of gradients for hill climbing with different sizes and weights of chassis, giving a limiting factor for those classes of vehicle with a very high back axle ratio that is unsuited to a very steep incline; for suspension testing over various conditions from a good main road to a country lane and the colonial type of road with potholes and ruts; and for experience to be obtained of steering stability and driving fatigue.

After making careful observations in various districts within easy reach of London, it was found that the best country for such tests was on the borders of Surrey and Kent, and eventually a route which has now been used for over 20 years, with the exception of the intervening war period, was decided upon. Covering a distance of approximately 45 miles, it begins at Croydon Airport on Purley Way, and passes through Purley, Caterham, Warlingham, Westerham, West Wickham and Shirley, thence returning to the starting point through Croydon.

This route is particularly favourable for passenger vehicles, and has been selected to provide suitable loops which can be traversed or omitted, according to the discretion of the tester and the type of machine undergoing test. For the greater part of its distance the course is covered by double and single-deck routes of the London Transport Executive, both Country and Central area, and it includes a short stretch of tramway in Croydon. It will be seen,

therefore, that this route is not in the nature of a freak course, but one composed mainly of ordinary roads.

All the machines road tested are standard production models of the road vehicle industry — prototypes and experimental designs being unacceptable for such purposes. It does speak well for this trial route, however, that almost as a matter of course manufacturers have adopted the practice of submitting new models for testing over the route immediately production commences. Through the limitation of body-building production and the possibility of accidental damage, passenger models are usually tested in chassis form with test weights attached to correspond to the designed load — ie body weight plus 1.5cwt per passenger. Before commencing the test each vehicle is taken to a weighbridge at Croydon, where the gross weight and the axle weights are obtained. The driver and observer are also included.

The first few miles of a test might be described as a preliminary canter when the tester gets the feel of the machine and also observes its general behaviour. Within a short distance one can prophesy fairly accurately the performance of the machine over the remainder of the course. The winding descent of the Caterham Bypass serves as an admirable stretch of road where the stability at speed with the counter effect of an induced swerving motion can be noted. A more accurate idea of the rolling motion set up is obtained with a vehicle complete with either a single or double-deck bus or coach body. Next comes the principal test hill, known as Succombs Hill, where the tests are always made against a stop-watch from a standing start. Its steepest part is 1 in 4.25 and might be considered too steep for the average public service vehicle, but when it is considered that there exist in these islands many bus routes which traverse some hills nearly as stiff, the test imposed must obviously be greater if the operator is to be given confidence in the performance.

In these tests the driver has ample opportunity of discovering all the good points in the vehicle he is handling and can observe such items as engine power and acceleration; action of clutch; ease of gear manipulation; engine vibration; and also overheating of engine or transmission. If there is a shortage of engine power, or indication of an unduly high gear ratio, it is useless to attempt Succombs Hill and a parallel hill with a gradient of 1 in 6 is tackled. Greatest demand made of the chassis is during the climbing of either of the two last-mentioned hills, when a stop and restart is attempted on the steepest slope. This requires not only full engine torque but an efficient and smooth transmission that will withstand the strain of this severe punishment.

The machine is run on full throttle along the ridge of Warlingham Heights to the top of Titsey Hill, a summit of 869ft, on the highest main road in the south of England. Here a very good brake fade test can then be made down the hill. This is done by coasting in neutral for a mile with a brake application to reduce the speed to 12mph, followed by an increase to 30mph at Titsey Church and a full application to ascertain the reaction of the heated brake drums and linings. It is not unusual for the linings to catch fire, Titsey Church being reached in clouds of blue smoke. After another mile of running the brakes are again applied to note how rapidly they are cooling off.

Some interesting test country is now encountered in a colonial loop through a water-splash and along a very rough surface where conditions are akin to those traversed by buses in many of the British Colonies. Controllability and suspension are the two points to be watched here; the irregular pattern of the roadway soon reveals any weakness in the steering gear. A very circuitous course from Limpsfield to Westerham soon makes the tester feel limp if the steering is heavy or the gears difficult to engage. After ascending Westerham Hill, the fuel test is carried out on a give and take route to Croydon. It is usually completed in two parts, the first being a nonstop run at a high average speed and the second including four intermediate stops in a mile to approximate to the work of a coach in heavy

traffic or a bus on local stage operation. Mitcham Common provides the level roads for braking tests and timing of acceleration, both through the gears and as a measure of torque in top gear from 10mph up to the maximum.

Sometimes 8ft-wide vehicles or over-length vehicles intended for export are taken over the route; the largest of these was a two-axle Dennis Lancet IV chassis intended for Sydney, New South Wales, and 34ft 8in long. It is remarkable how easily such vehicles traverse the narrowest country lanes and sharpest corners, and how easily manoeuvrable they prove to be in the busy streets of crowded Croydon. They afford still more proof, if that were needed, that our vehicle regulations are unduly restricted by the Ministry of Transport.

The final stage of these independent tests is the compilation of an accurate and frank report and the production of a table of the results of observed tests easy to read and understand. This provides the operator with a means to assess the capabilities of a vehicle under conditions which are, perhaps, not quite as extreme as the searching tests of the manufacturers' research departments, but rigid enough to ensure that the vehicle is perfectly efficient for service at home or abroad. From experiences over the test course which has been described with a wide range of passenger chassis, it is gratifying to be aware of the successful manner in which our British vehicles master a hard task.

John H. Fielder, Road Test Engineer of Modern Transport, *writing in* Buses and Trams, *published by Ian Allan Ltd in 1949.*

Below: A Dennis Lancet IV chassis is seen on test in early 1949. Another feature of the tests in the trade press was the number of chassis types destined for the export market that were examined. The Lancet IV was an export version of the postwar Lancet J3, but had a 21ft 6in wheelbase to accommodate bodies of up to 36ft in length.

This road test of the AEC Regent double-deck bus is the first of a new series, in which the technical value of the observations recorded is increased as vehicles are now being taken direct from road service, operated either by municipal or private undertakings, or by goods haulage firms, and driven under test conditions round the *Modern Transport* circuit in Derbyshire by our Chief Road Transport Vehicle Tester and under observation of the representatives of the operating companies and the manufacturers respectively. In this particular instance, AEC arranged with Mr C. H. Stafford, General Manager of the Burnley Corporation Tramways & Omnibuses, for one of the Corporation buses to be driven to Buxton for test purposes, under the observation of Mr Stafford himself and one of their own representatives, as, in view of the nature of the test and the conditions of the route, they considered that valuable information would be derived from the procedure.

Having studied the proposed test route from descriptions previously published in *Modern Transport*, and as no double-deck vehicle had hitherto undergone a trial over the circuit, Mr Stafford suggested that a party consisting of himself, a representative of AEC and our Chief Tester should inspect the course fully on the day prior to the actual test to ascertain whether a standard bus could be driven all round without risking damage to the upper deck. This proved to be a wise precaution, as two low railway bridges were found to necessitate slight detours, but these in no way detracted from the general characteristics of the route, and by a fortunate coincidence, brought in gradients to substitute those that had to be bypassed, and gave a total mileage exactly equal to that of the normal test circuit.

The AEC Regent double-deck bus submitted for test was placed in service by Burnley Corporation in early April 1932, and had already covered well over 12,000 miles. A total weight equivalent to that of 51 passengers was disposed, in the form of bags of cement, under the seats of the saloon and upper deck of the body, which was built to Burnley Corporation specifications by Charles Roe Ltd, of Crossgates, Leeds. This weight and that of four extra passengers, comprising Mr Stafford, his Rolling Stock Superintendent, Mr Applegate of Oswald Tillotsons and our representative, constituted an overload.

Ease of Control

In accordance with our usual practice, we took charge of the vehicle at the start of the test run from Buxton, the highest town in England, and proceeded along the busy thoroughfare of Spring Gardens towards Ashwood Dale. Here, as at many other parts of the route, we found it necessary to exercise extreme caution to avoid overhanging trees, but we derived great assistance from the services of the 'look-out' man on the upper deck, who rang the bell when danger threatened. Even when driving a bare chassis over this route, one gets a very definite opinion as to controllability, which, needless to say, is greatly emphasised in the case of a fully loaded double-decker. The Regent, however, gave no cause for anxiety on this score, as the faultless steering and the ample flexibility provided by the 95hp six-cylinder

Right: **The very first AEC Regent, chassis No 661001 (the 661 referred to the chassis type), was built in the summer of 1929. The new model had a wheelbase of 15ft 6.5in and was fitted with an AEC six-cylinder petrol engine.**

engine inspired confidence that was destined to stand us in good stead throughout the journey round the famous Peak District. To our great relief, we found the gears quick and easy to manipulate, and it was not long before we became thoroughly accustomed to changing up and down under the driving conditions imposed by a full load in the upper and lower passenger compartments. The braking system, also, left nothing to be desired. At Kingsterndale, where bridge building was in progress, we were forced down to a very moderate pace and crept beneath suspiciously low girders with the knowledge of having a few necessary inches to spare. We then commenced the long climb up Topley Pike to mountain altitudes, where the road traverses bleak moorland.

Referring to the subject of route gradients tackled by this vehicle, which is normally employed on town service, Mr Stafford told us afterwards that none of those we encountered during the journey were any more severe than the inclines traversed regularly on the Burnley routes, so that in some respects the Regent was only called upon to demonstrate its usual performance in a highly concentrated form, without the relief afforded by intermittent travel on level roads. Mr Stafford also agreed with our description of the test as being one that gives a vehicle no respite from start to finish of the course. Our first observations on the ample reserve of power provided by the engine

Left: **One of a batch of Cowieson-bodied AEC Regents supplied to the Northern Ireland Road Transport Board in 1938 undergoes a tilt test. The hydraulic tilting table stands at 28°; the vehicle, as a result of spring deflection, stands at 35° off the vertical.**

Above: A batch of exported AEC Regents is seen being bodied at the Waddington bodyworks in Sydney, Australia, in early 1938. The order, for 50 chassis (later increased to 55), was placed in July 1937 and at the time represented the largest single order received by AEC from Australia.

Left: Photographed at the Pier in 1963 is Douglas Corporation's last prewar AEC Regent No 50. This vehicle was new in 1939 and was fitted with a Northern Counties body. On withdrawal it was preserved and reregistered SWU222F. *David Stuttard*

were made during the early stages of the climb to Taddington Moor, past Sough Top (1,437ft above sea level), as the Regent put in some excellent work on third gear, before the gradient became more severe, when a run of 1min 35sec duration in second gear brought us to the summit. Then came the steep and winding descent through Taddington village, where, to save the brake linings, the engine was used for braking purposes against third gear. Incidentally, it may be mentioned that after having been in use for over 12,000 miles, the third gear was very smooth and quiet in action, both while transmitting the drive and on the over-run, when the stresses on the gear teeth are reversed. The run down Taddington Dale enabled

us to travel at a good cruising speed, 40mph being reached occasionally, and the easier curves in the road were taken quite fast without there being the slightest tendency for the big vehicle to sway or become unmanageable. After negotiating the acute corners in Ashford, we continued up and down the series of hills and ran into Bakewell, having averaged 20mph over this relatively difficult portion of the route, which is known locally as the 'Road of the Seven Hills'.

Ample Engine Power

At Bakewell we turned from the ordinary route past Haddon Hall, through Great Rowsley and Chatsworth Park, a picturesque part of the run denied to double-deck buses by the builders of the low railway bridge at Great Rowsley, to pick up the ordinary course again a little to the south of Baslow. Here we encountered a herd of cattle, which caused us to make an unpremeditated stop-and-restart test on an awkward incline, but the Regent made light of the incident and picked up speed readily, so that we were soon travelling along the steadily rising road to Calver and thence to Grindleford Bridge. At the last-named place, a knowledge of the course is very beneficial, for just as

one is making a gentle descent on top gear, there is a sharp turn to the left and almost before there is time to drop into second gear, a sharp ascent, known as School Hill (1 in 5), comes into view. On this occasion we were ready with the gears and the Regent showed its admirable controllability by permitting us to effect a snap change into first gear after negotiating the acute turn, which enabled us to make a very effective climb in 1min 20sec, with plenty of power in reserve. This was the only occasion when first gear was needed throughout the whole run.

From Grindleford to Hathersage, the narrow road is bordered by Sherriff Wood on the left, and by the River Derwent on the opposite side, but we were unable to enjoy the scenery at this very picturesque part of the run owing to the repeated warnings of our 'look-out' man, whose bell reminded us that bough-dodging evaluations were again necessary. Both the railway bridges at Hathersage provide a clear passage for double-deckers, provided that the man at the wheel steers accurately for the arch centres, although the approach to the first may cause some misgivings owing to the steep rise leading to the village. The next interesting part of the run is at Bamford, a little village built on a steep hill known as 'Great Tor'. Judging from the performance of other vehicles tested over this route, we anticipated a spell of second gear work to negotiate the climb through the narrow street, but the Regent gave us a pleasant surprise by gliding up on third gear, and, although the engine was forced down to a very low speed, it continued to exert such even and powerful torque that no change down was needed, and we were still travelling on this ratio at Ashopton, where the main Sheffield-Manchester road is joined, and where travel becomes more and more arduous as the difficult Snake Pass is approached.

One of the practical advantages of employing a comparatively short, but strenuous, route for these tests is that the journey can be covered without a stop, which, besides limiting the time a vehicle is out of service for test purposes, increases the severity of the test conditions. Thus, before the timed ascent of Snake Pass is commenced, there are ample opportunities for latent engine defects to develop, should such exist. The lubricating system must be perfect to maintain an adequate supply of oil to the vital parts of the engine, which has to work at high speed for long periods, and if there should be any defect in the cooling system, there will be distinct possibilities of cylinder head distortion. The valve mechanism must be beyond reproach if it is to stand up to the relentless 'revving' required of the engine at various stages of the test. Again, the brakes, which must be used frequently for long periods, are not allowed time to cool down during stoppages, and altogether the vehicle is called upon to withstand much harder work in a space of a few hours than is imposed by several days of regular work under normal service conditions. Therefore a nonstop run at a reasonably high speed over such a course as is being described, provides all the elements of a genuine test, which are not so well provided when stops are permitted.

Adequate Fuel Supply

It will be realised that had any latent fault existed in the Regent it would certainly have been revealed during the long climb over the Snake Pass, where the roadway rises to a height of 1,680ft above sea level. At this part of the route the country is wild in the extreme, with Kinder Scout, the highest part of the Peak District, on the left and the rugged heights of Allport Moor on the right. The road surface here, as in all other parts of the test circuit is excellent, and the Regent began the arduous run of 13 miles from Ashopton to Glossop by climbing smoothly on third

gear with intermittent spells of top gear towards Gillithey Farm Bridge, where the timed climb of the Snake begins. Halfway between the bridge and the summit we passed the Snake Inn on top gear at 25mph, and thence the gradient increases and third gear was required to negotiate the 'S' bend at Birchin Bridge, which only just permits the passage of a large double-decker. Still climbing over Clough Moor, the bus maintained a steady rate of progress, and after a short run on second gear the summit was reached after a climb of 4.5 miles in 14min 41sec, during which the engine ran without a moment's hesitation and without any interruption to the fuel supply, the consumption of petrol being low enough to obviate any starving of the vacuum feed tank. The long run on second gear was accomplished without causing the radiator to overheat, and the temperature within the cab was not unduly oppressive. Incidentally, we were greatly impressed by the absence of valve gear noise when the engine was running at high speed under full load.

Looking in a westerly direction from the Snake summit, one gets a good view of Glossop and Oldham, before starting the 4.5-mile descent to the first-named place, along the winding road skirting the edge of the precipitous

drop on the left. On more than one occasion we have passed vehicles stopped for brake adjustments on this part of the course, but the Regent brakes appeared to be just as effective as they were at the start, which gave us confidence in making the descent of over 1,000ft into Glossop. With only 16.5 miles to complete the journey from Glossop to Buxton, after passing over the part of the route already described, one naturally anticipates a somewhat easier run over the last stage of the test, but as Buxton is situated at a height of over 1,000ft above sea level and mountain heights separate the low-lying towns between Glossop and the finishing point, the final stage of the journey is actually more severe than the preceding portions, not even excluding the Snake section.

A Long Climb

From Glossop to Hayfield, for example, there is the long climb over Chunal Moor, where the roadway

Right: **Cardiff corporation No 8 was one of a batch of 10 50-seat diesel-engined AEC Regents supplied in 1934. The bodywork was supplied by Northern Counties. Nine of the batch, including No 8, were rebodied by East Lancs in 1944. The vehicle, renumbered 31 in 1949, was withdrawn for scrap the following year.**

15

rises to 1,057ft, but the Regent continued to pull valiantly on third gear to the top. Double-deckers escape another long climb over Chinley Head into Chapel-en-le-Frith, which has to be bypassed to miss the low railway bridge near Chapel Milon, and pass through the town of New Mills to join the Stockport-Buxton road by a very acute hairpin bend on an upward incline near Newton railway station. Although there is very little roadway width to spare at this difficult turn, the Regent took it easily on full lock in third gear and pulled away with remarkable readiness. After leaving Whaley Bridge, we began the final climb up Long Hill, which takes a tortuous course between mountain heights, the road rising to 1,250ft, before dropping into Buxton. This final stretch of uphill work was mastered on third gear, so that in the 59-mile course, second gear was only used for 11min 51sec and first gear on one occasion only for 1min 20sec.

Above: Originally numbered 243 in the Leeds Corporation fleet, this 1938 AEC Regent, fitted with Roe 56-seat bodywork, passed to Barton in 1950 following withdrawal. As Barton No 644, the bus was to survive in service until July 1961. It is seen at Barton's Ilkeston depot shortly after withdrawal. *Michael Fowler*

Although no attempt was made to complete the run at anything over ordinary cruising speed, the average worked out at just over 21mph, which gives a very good idea of the vehicle's capabilities over what is admittedly a very severe course. We are glad to be able to state that Mr Charles Stafford considers the route to be a perfectly fair one, even for a double-decker, and one that will certainly bring out all the good points in any vehicle, as well as reveal any directions in which imperfections may exist. He also added that he would have no hesitation in regarding this test as one providing a standard of performance for municipal and other road vehicles. From the various observations recorded above it is clear that the Regent completed the test in a way that should uphold its reputation among municipal transport users. Reference must also be made to the high standard of coachwork fitted to the chassis by Charles Roe Ltd. Furthermore, the fact that the run was accomplished without the need for adjustment of any kind indicates the first-class maintenance on the part of the operators, and the Burnley Tramways & Omnibuses are undoubtedly entitled to share with AEC in the credit for the vehicle having put up a performance which sets a very high standard in every way.

Update

The vehicle used in the test, Burnley No 39 (HG1025), passed to Burnley, Colne & Nelson Joint Transport in 1933. It was one of a batch of eight vehicles of the type bought by Burnley in 1932, but was destined to have a much shorter life than the remainder, being destroyed in a fire at Colne depot in 1937. The other seven were withdrawn between 1945 and 1950. The AEC Regent was one of the most successful of bus designs introduced prior to World War 2. Over 7,000 were constructed between 1929 — when the chassis was launched — and the end of production during the war. In addition, the chassis was also modified as the basis of the prewar LTPB RT-type. Initially the chassis had a wheelbase of 15ft 6.5in, but this was lengthened to 16ft 3in in 1931; at the same time a diesel engine option was also offered.

General Data

Engine:	Six-cylinder with 100mm bore and 130mm stroke. Volume, 6.25litre. Maximum bhp, 95. RAC rating, 37.2mph. Average fuel consumption, 0.6pints per bhp/hr
Clutch:	Single dry plate. Diameter of plate, 16in. Area of friction surfaces, 180sq in
Gearbox:	Number of forward gears, four. First gear ratio: 4.47 to 1 Second gear ratio: 2.70 to 1 Third gear ratio: 1.59 to 1 Fourth gear ratio: Direct Reverse: 5.33 to 1
Rear Axle:	Underslung worm. Semi-floating. Ratio, 6.25 to 1 with alternative of 7.33 to 1
Brakes:	Foot, operated by vacuum servo on four wheels. Hand, on rear wheels only
Chassis:	Wheelbase 15ft 6.5in. Track (front), 6ft 3.0625in. Track (rear), 5ft 10.1875in. Overall length, 24ft 10.875in. Frame length behind dash, 20ft in. Ground clearance up to rear axle, 10in. Frame width, 3ft 11.625in. Turning circle, 57ft. Maximum speed, 40mph. Weight of chassis, 3ton 5cwt.

In accordance with their usual practice when introducing a new series of vehicles, the Associated Equipment Co Ltd of Southall recently placed one of the first of their new AEC-Ricardo oil-engined Q bus chassis at the disposal of *Modern Transport* for test over our southern route, this being the first occasion upon which a trial of the new model has been carried out except by the manufacturers themselves. The chassis submitted was one destined for luxury passenger service as a single-deck coach, and it arrived at the Aerodrome Hotel, Purley Way, Croydon in chassis form carrying test weights representing the total passenger load, plus the usual bodywork allowance. At the start of the test run the chassis had only covered 140 miles, which meant that the hard driving to which models are usually submitted when undergoing these trials had to be tempered to some extent. It will be quite safe to assume, therefore, that a considerable improvement in the performance

recorded should be obtainable from vehicles of the new series after they have been in service for a few weeks.

Apart from the new AEC-Ricardo oil engine fitted to this model, the chassis is equipped with the fluid flywheel manufactured at Southall under Daimler licence and a pre-selective gearbox also produced at the AEC Works under licence of Improved Gears Ltd. A further point of interest is that the bands working on the epicyclic gear drums are now provided with grooves instead of being plain, which is said to present definite advantages to the operator. The new engine is certainly more quiet than the earlier units, both at idling speeds and when pulling under full load, whilst recent modifications have resulted in even better fuel consumption than before. During the short run from the Aerodrome Hotel to the starting point of the first observed section of the route, we were able to renew our acquaintance with the control of the Q chassis, which was first made while testing a petrol-driven model over the same route last year, the results being published in the 4 November issue of *Modern Transport*. The vehicle created a good impression in all respects, particularly as to ease of control, power and acceleration, the behaviour of the fluid transmission providing a standard of driving comfort that certainly cannot be attained with any form of conventional gearing.

Easy Running and Good Acceleration

By virtue of its small turning circle, the chassis was swung round without reversing in the roadway at

Below: **There were just under 350 AEC Q chassis manufactured, of which all but 23 were single-deck. Of the total built, more than two-thirds were operated by London Transport. This manufacturer's photograph of No Q7 shows clearly the grille associated with the offside-mounted engine. No Q7 was the second of the production batch of type designated by the LPTB 4Q4; these were Nos Q6-Q105 and Q186/187. Bodywork was by the Birmingham Carriage & Wagon Co.**

Waddon railway station, and we then proceeded towards Purley Way to try the capabilities of the latest AEC-Ricardo engine as it pulled the fully-loaded chassis up to the trying ascent which leads up and passes the London airport. This climb began with the vehicle travelling on top gear at 25mph, after which it accelerated freely and passed the aerodrome at an easy 35mph. Still producing plenty of power, the engine continued to pull smoothly and quietly, without calling for third gear even when the summit was approached, the climb finishing at a speed of 25mph on top gear. In view of the 5.4 to 1 final reduction, this was a particularly encouraging performance. The next observations were directed to easy running of the chassis as it was allowed to coast in neutral from the crest of Purley Way to the Brighton road, when, by virtue of the mechanical refinements of the transmission system, it ran with absolute silence and smoothness. A test of the brakes under normal driving conditions proved satisfactory for, at 30mph, an application of the vacuum-assisted brakes produced the desired retardation with the minimum amount of effort.

Exceptionally good acceleration was noted as we moved off after a traffic stop at Purley crossroads, when the new AEC-Ricardo oil engine revealed some of its qualities. The unit has a total volume of 7.4litres and, measuring 106mm bore by 156mm stroke, is capable of developing 126bhp at the maximum governing speed of 2,400rpm. The cylinders are fitted with hardened renewable liners and the cylinder heads are in RR50 alloy, in accordance with standard AEC practice for oil engines, the usual valves and the AEC-Ricardo combustion chamber being incorporated. In this new engine the valves are operated by means of short push rods from the camshaft, which is carried in a tunnel cored in the cylinder block, thus permitting a very short and simple chain lay-out, and effecting a considerable reduction in weight.

A Hill Test

The usual tests for suspension and ease of steering over uneven surfaces were applied at Whyteleafe, when the admirable balance of the chassis and the action of the long and wide springs enabled the vehicle to hold the road with commendable ease. The common tendency for models undergoing test to wander over this part of the course was totally absent. Omitting Succombs Hill (1 in 4.5) on account of the high final reduction used for single-deck Q models,

we proceeded from Caterham Valley to Warlingham Heights via Bug Hill (1 in 6), which offers a fairer test in such circumstances. Several very acute corners had to be negotiated before reaching the steepest part of the incline, but the Q chassis proved easy to handle along the narrow winding road. As we approached the ascent the vehicle was proceeding on third gear, but second was already pre-selected in readiness for a quick gear change likely to be needed as the gradient became more severe. Just before reaching the 1 in 6 portion, the necessary movement of the gear-operating pedal was made, and then the climb was completed in excellent style with a sufficient power reserve to prevent any anxiety. The performance on this difficult hill demonstrated the efficiency of the transmission, which was free from the least inclination to slip, even under the most exacting route conditions.

The course continued through Upper Warlingham, and on leaving the village we allowed the chassis to run for a short distance at full speed along that part of the road where fast travel is possible. Holding the road comfortably, the Q chassis proceeded at 52mph, which did not appear to represent the ultimate speed to be expected when in a thoroughly run-in condition, in which circumstances it is quite probable that a speed of 60mph should be possible. At Worms Heath the chassis gave another notable performance by surmounting the first of the gradients on top gear at 40mph, after which — unlike most vehicles tested over this route — the remaining gradients were mastered on the same ratio, which gave a finishing speed of 20mph as the final observation point was passed.

Westerham Hill

The footbrake operates on all four wheels by a servo-assisted hydraulic system, which has the advantage of being automatically self-adjusting. The large single

Above left: Another 4Q4 was No Q13 pictured here at Kingston. The 4Q4 type was allocated by the LPTB to Country Area services. *F. G. Reynolds*

Above: This interior shot of 5Q5 No Q113 shows that the seating capacity for this model was 37.

Right: One of the later 5Q5 type, No Q174, is seen in Welling. There were 80 members of the 5Q5 type, Nos Q106-185, all of which were originally designed for use on Central Area routes, although 27 were actually allocated to the Country Area. Bodywork this time was by Park Royal and the 5Q5 had a shorter wheelbase than the 4Q4. *F. G. Reynolds*

Below right:
The 50 Q types delivered to Green Line, Nos Q189-Q238, were designated 6Q6 by the LPTB. No Q209 is pictured in Portland Place. During the war these vehicles operated as ambulances, reverting to Green Line use after the cessation of hostilities. *F. G. Reynolds*

shoes on the rear axle are, in addition, operated by the handbrake. These features were put to test whilst descending Titsey Hill (1 in 6), when the vehicle was allowed to travel down the steep incline at 30mph before the brakes were applied at the maximum gradient. At this point a steady pressure on the pedal brought the chassis down to a walking pace with an agreeably progressive retardation. Further tests were applied with the objective of heating up the drums, but even when applied with warmed drums the braking system was equally effective. After proceeding through Limpsfield on top gear we swept round the sharp corner at the end of the village on third and climbed up on to the Godstone-Westerham road, when travel became easier over undulating roads before Westerham was reached.

On leaving Westerham the Q chassis gave a striking demonstration of ease and quickness in control as a sharp and narrow turn is encountered on entering the London road from the Square. The chance of obstructing vehicles coming from the opposite direction at this point increases the need of ready manoeuvre, in which respect the Q chassis merited the highest praise. The steering gear, incidentally, is of the worm and nut type, embodying the dual purpose ball-bearing mounted at the top of the steering column, which is insulated from road shock by a patented type of mounting. The very deceptive approach to Westerham Hill, where the road, although apparently level, invariably calls for a steady pull on third gear, causes a considerable reduction in the speed for the timed climb up this gradient. The Q bus chassis traversed the crossroads at 19mph on third gear, but second had already been pre-selected for engagement some 50yd higher up. The bottom ratio was not reached until the first bend (1 in 6) was reached, and thence to near the summit a minimum speed of 8mph was maintained. Finally, the timing point was passed on third gear at 20mph, the climb having occupied 3min 19sec.

Acceleration and Braking

Further information concerning performance was provided by the series of acceleration and braking tests which took place on a straight, level stretch of road near the finishing point of the timed climb. The first acceleration test consisted of starting the chassis on top gear and attaining a speed of 30mph without engaging any of the lower ratios. This test was of special interest as it showed the ability of the fluid flywheel to deal with the full load, through a high final reduction, without revealing the slightest indication of undue slip, the required road speed being attained in 21sec. As the result of the next acceleration test, the speed was reached in 15sec from a standing start, the four forward ratios being engaged progressively in the usual manner. This also proved very enlightening on account of the remarkable rapidity with which the gears could be operated, due to the facility for pre-selection. The final test for rolling acceleration from 10mph to 30mph on top gear occupied 17.4sec, the whole series providing conclusive evidence of the ability of the Q chassis to satisfy all conditions likely to be met in passenger service.

In travelling round the hilly route, the vehicle had fully satisfied all demands for brake efficiency and durability, but further brake tests were applied for comparative purposes. Thus, when proceeding at 30mph on a level road, we applied the footbrake, which brought the chassis smoothly to rest in exactly 4sec. The handbrake, employed normally for parking, when applied at the same speed arrested the motion of the vehicle in 6.8sec. Finally, to observe the action of the brakes and the behaviour of the chassis under emergency stop conditions, a speed of 30mph was again attained and then both brakes were operated suddenly to the fullest possible extent, which stopped the vehicle in 3.8sec without producing the slightest deviation from a true course or causing any of the wheels to lock. Having completed the observed portions of the course, the chassis was submitted to further tests for hill climbing ability, including an ascent of Salt Box Hill, the zigzag at West Wickham, and other gradients on the way back to Croydon, where the test was brought to a satisfactory

conclusion after having satisfied all conditions imposed by a particularly searching route.

Update

The AEC Q was launched in September 1932. A total of 319 single-deck chassis were completed before production ceased in 1938. It was possible to obtain both petrol and diesel engined versions, these being designated 762 and 0762 respectively. A double-deck version was launched in 1934, with a total of 23 being built. The most numerous operator of the Q-type was the LPTB, but a number also found their way to provincial operators. A small number survive in preservation.

Above: A fascinating scene in Aberdeen — just look at the period detail including on the extreme left the steam lorry — sees Aberdeen Q-type No 105 in 1936. Aberdeen acquired its first Q in 1934 (No 21) and a further 10 (Nos 22-31) the following year. A further two, Nos 104/05, were acquired when the business of Rover Bus Service was taken over on 14 November 1935. Nos 104/105 were new in 1934 and were fitted with rear-entrance Walker 34-seat bodywork.

Below: One of the last AEC Q-type chassis to survive in service was this 35-seat coach supplied to Silver Service of Darley Dale in 1934. It was fitted with a Willowbrook body and was preserved on withdrawal. The front end was modified with the appearance of a radiator grille during its operational career.

Because of the remote situation of the Bristol Tramway & Carriage Co's works at Brislington, Bristol, in relation to either of the *Modern Transport* test routes, their latest single-deck omnibus chassis was tested by our representative recently over the company's own circuit, which including some of the severe gradients of the Mendip Hills, serves for the final road tests before Bristol models are put into service. The model submitted to test was a standard JO5G unit fitted with a five-cylinder Gardner oil engine and the Bristol five-speed gearbox, and it carried test weights representing the full load of 32 passengers, a driver, a conductor, and a body allowance.

On taking charge of the vehicle at the Brislington Works, we began the test by driving it along the main Bristol-Bath road, when its general performance revealed ample engine power, lively acceleration, and ease and convenience of control. The five-cylinder oil engine is placed well forward in the frame to allow the maximum room for passengers, and is mounted on frame brackets with rubber insulation, thus damping out any excessive vibration. The Gardner engine (4.5in bore and 6in stroke) develops its maximum of 85bhp at 1,700rpm, and, with suitably selected normal gear ratios and an overspeed top gear, appears to be fully capable of satisfying all service conditions. Ease of gear manipulation is certainly one of the features to be found in this chassis, this resulting from the smooth action of the single-plate clutch, actuated by pedal pressure of about 35lb, and the short, easy movements required to operate the gear-selector mechanism. The clutch, by the way, is designed to stand disengagement for long periods of 'coasting' without suffering wear on the withdrawal mechanism, a practice encouraged on the Bristol bus services to the exclusion of 'coasting' in neutral.

Effect of Overspeed Gear

Engagement of the direct top gear, transmitting the engine power to the 6 in 1 rear axle, enabled us to negotiate the rising gradient towards Keynsham at an easy 30mph, and, later, by a quick side and forward movement of the single-selector lever, the fifth, or overspeed, gear, giving a ratio of 0.695 to 1, was brought into action. The effect of this overspeed gear is remarkable, as it allows the engine to 'tick over' while propelling the vehicle at a good speed with smooth and quiet motion.

A very good castoring action and light control characterise the steering gear, which provides a turning circle of 58ft 6in, and works through worm and quadrant gears mounted on taper roller bearings. Attention was next directed to the behaviour of the

brakes and the value of the engine for retardation purposes while descending a long and gradual incline, which served also for a simple test of tractive resistance. For the latter, the selector lever was slipped into the neutral position, thus allowing the chassis to 'coast' freely for a short distance. This test proved quite satisfactory, in that the entire transmission was free from undue friction, and we could detect no louder sound than the hissing of the tyres on the road. When running under normal conditions, also, the model is notably free from transmission noises, largely by reason of the silently-acting helical constant mesh gears.

Brake and Suspension Tests

At 30mph a gentle application of the footbrake brought the chassis to rest with a smooth action in 3.6sec, while the handbrake proved equally effective. The lever is situated conveniently for use in service, though operated normally for parking purposes only. When in the 'off' position, it is prevented from vibrating by means of a spring steel retaining clip

Below left: **This was one of a batch of 10 Bristol JJW vehicles supplied to Eastern Counties in mid-1935. The vehicles were fitted with ECW 32-seat bodies. No LJ5 was renumbered LJ435 in 1946 and was withdrawn in 1956.**

Below: **The Bristol/Gardner combination featured in the** *Modern Transport* **road test of December 1934. The weather conditions look particularly unpleasant for a test in late December, particularly given the lack of protection afforded to both the test driver and observer.**

attached to the side of the bonnet. The brakes on all four wheels have single shoes operated simultaneously by the pedal, assisted by a master Dewandre servo connected to the rear brakes. The front brakes are applied by two cylinders mounted on the pivot axles and controlled by the master servo. Ample braking area is provided by the 17.25in alloy cast-iron drums and the wide shoes, which are 6in wide for the front drums and 7.5in for the rear, all shoes being adjustable without removing the brake drums. The handbrake operates upon the shoes in the rear wheel drums through independent linkage. When travelling at the maximum speed the footbrake brought the chassis to rest in 3.8sec without the least trace of skid or wheel lock.

A section of the route where road reconstruction operations were in progress, when traversed at speeds varying between 10 and 40mph, served for a particularly searching test of the entire suspension system. The springs proved fully capable of absorbing all road shocks without suffering undue oscillations, with the result that the rear wheels maintained a continuous rolling action while transmitting the drive evenly over the rough surface. The behaviour of the front axle suspension was equally good, and no shocks or vibrations were transferred from the road wheels to the driver's hands through the steering column. The suspension arrangement incorporates a Bristol patent, the springs being shackled to the frame brackets, but the bushes do not carry the load, their sole purpose being to keep the springs in position. The actual load is taken by cam-shaped brackets attached to the frame, these being so arranged that, as the load increases, the effective length of the springs is reduced. By this means it is possible to employ very flexible springs for

light and normal loads without incurring any risk of damage from overloads.

Hill Climbing

Turning from the main road after having travelled a few miles in the direction of Bath, we proceeded towards the Mendip Hills in order to test the chassis for hill climbing ability near Chelwood. Here a gradient of 1 in 8, in addition to affording a good opportunity for a test of full engine power, permitted observations as to the selection of the gear ratios, clutch action, and general ease of control. A start was made on second gear and very lively acceleration produced the speed necessary for engagement of the third ratio, upon which the engine pulled strongly until the maximum gradient of 1 in 8 was reached.

Then came a quick drop back into second gear, when the engine displayed an ample reserve of power, by aid of which the chassis surmounted the remainder of the hill in a style which was eminently satisfactory.

The next portion of the route was of particular interest, since it consisted of a number of winding roads where easy steering, quick brakes, and rapid acceleration were in almost continuous demand. In all these details the Bristol chassis satisfied every demand, and proved itself fully capable of good performance in town traffic work, where such qualities are needed perhaps to an even greater extent. At its maximum speed, with the overspeed gear ratio in action, the Bristol chassis travelled with all the smoothness of a high-grade touring car, and appeared to be quite able to maintain a steady 48mph, should road and traffic conditions permit.

Acceleration Tests

The usual series of acceleration tests was very interesting, especially in view of the relatively low power developed by the five-cylinder oil engine, for the results obtained compared very favourably with those of an average six-cylinder chassis of similar carrying capacity. The first test consisted of starting the chassis from rest with the top normal gear engaged, and attaining the legal speed of 30mph in the shortest time possible with the minimum amount of initial clutch slip and no further engagement of the indirect ratios, or slipping of the clutch. It is obvious, of course, that a standing start test in top gear imposes severe momentary stresses upon the engine, clutch and transmission alike, but it was accomplished in a most satisfactory manner, the drive being taken up with complete freedom from snatch or other irregularities, and the required speed being attained in exactly 26sec.

For the second acceleration test, the same speed was gained in 24sec after starting away in bottom gear in the ordinary way and going through the box to engage each gear in turn. Here, very considerable benefit was derived from the quick and easy action of the Bristol patent single-rod selector control, by the aid of which it is possible to pick up the required gears directly the engine speed is right, thus obtaining rapid and silent gear changes. The final test for rolling acceleration from 10mph to 30mph on top gear occupied only 15sec, during which time the engine exerted a smooth and powerful torque over the required speed range, while displaying an almost unexpected degree of flexibility.

Thus it will be seen that the five-cylinder Gardner-engined Bristol chassis, with full load, satisfies all conditions likely to be demanded in town and country services, while its all-round performance conforms with the highest standards. The journey back to Brislington over an exceptionally hilly route provided further tests of durability, and gave definite proof that the many mechanical refinements incorporated in the design are of practical value in enhancing the performance of this very advanced example of modern bus construction.

Update

The Bristol JO5G was launched in 1934 when a Gardner 5LW diesel engine was offered as an alternative to the Bristol JW petrol engine offered previously. The Bristol J-type was first launched in 1933 and the petrol-engined chassis were classified JJW after 1934. Although these were the two main power unit options, others were also available. Production of the J-type ceased in 1937, when it was replaced by the L-type. More than 900 J-types were built, but only a handful survive into preservation.

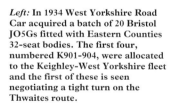

Left: In 1934 West Yorkshire Road Car acquired a batch of 20 Bristol JO5Gs fitted with Eastern Counties 32-seat bodies. The first four, numbered K901-904, were allocated to the Keighley-West Yorkshire fleet and the first of these is seen negotiating a tight turn on the Thwaites route.

Above right: This Bristol JJW was one of a batch supplied to Royal Blue in 1934/35. It was fitted with an ECW 32-seat coach body, a six-cylinder engine, four-speed gearbox with overdrive and luggage space in the roof.

Right: Delivered as No J168 in 1935, this Bristol Tramways & Carriage Co Bristol J was fitted with a Bristol 32-seat body. Renumbered 2033 in 1937, the vehicle was withdrawn in 1954. *D. W. Backhouse*

Dennis Lancet Coach

The 'Lancet' coach produced by Dennis Bros Ltd, and equipped with their 'Big 4' petrol engine and overspeed gearbox, certainly confounds those critics who maintain the absolute need of six-cylinder engines for long distance coaches, limited stop omnibuses, or any form of passenger vehicle other than buses operating over easy town routes. At one time there may have been good reasons for such views, but having developed the four-cylinder engine to a highly advanced stage, Dennis Bros have brought this more simple and less expensive form of power unit into great esteem amongst passenger vehicle operators.

The coach submitted for test over the *Modern Transport* Southern route was a vehicle which had already covered 20,000 miles on demonstration service in various parts of the country, and was therefore in representative condition for undergoing a series of strenuous trials. Arranged beneath the seats of the Dennis-built coachwork were weights equivalent to the normal complement of passengers, and the test started as usual from the Aerodrome Hotel, Purley Way, Croydon. Having already driven a Dennis coach fitted with the manufacturer's own gearbox, which gives an 'overspeed' or fifth ratio of 0.69 to 1, we were already familiar with the method of driving by which the maximum benefits of this transmission are obtained.

The Engine

The power unit, with bore and stroke dimensions of 120mm by 150mm respectively, is of sturdy compact design, and has overhead valves operated by push rods from a normally situated camshaft. Rated at 3.5 by RAC formula, it develops a maximum of no less than 97bhp at 2,000rpm, an output resulting from careful attention to all details of design. We have no hesitation in affirming that this four-cylinder engine compares very favourably with the average six-cylinder unit with regard to smooth operation and freedom from vibration, besides ensuring economy in fuel consumption, and simplifying maintenance. In brief, the power unit is fully capable of first class performance under any conceivable service condition, which is confirmed by our test results.

Operated by a large-diameter and conveniently arranged wheel, the worm and trunnion steering has a finger-light, self-centring action and a turning circle of 62ft. Very light pedal pressure is required to actuate the double-plate dry clutch, which presents the generous frictional area of 429sq in. Its quick and positive action in conjunction with the free movement of the gear selector mechanism renders gear-changing easy and silent at all times. Forming a single unit with the engine and fully enclosed clutch, the five-speed gearbox provides the following ratios: First, 5.19 to 1; second, 2.94 to 1; third, 1.55 to 1; top, direct and fifth, the overspeed ratio, is 0.69 to 1. These ratios, with a final reduction of 5.6 to 1 by Dennis underslung worm-gearing, provide well-graded 'steps' for any main road gradient, whilst ensuring adequate speeds and fuel economy.

General Performance

Satisfied with our preliminary observations, we started the test proper by trying the model for general performance whilst ascending the long incline at Purley Way. Traversing the Croydon-Sutton cross-roads with an initial speed of 20mph on top normal ratio, the Lancet accelerated freely towards the

Left: **Pictured during the actual** *Modern Transport* **test, the Dennis Lancet's brake drum temperatures are recorded.**

aerodrome, which was passed at 30mph. Although the gradient becomes increasingly steep towards the summit, the engine continued to pull smoothly on top gear, without the slightest inclination to 'pink' or detonate, thus proving that the automatic ignition control actuated by vacuum mechanism from the induction system was doing its work properly. By finishing this first climb at a speed of 30mph, this equalling average six-cylinder coach performance, the Lancet gave every promise of good results over parts of the circuit where more searching tests for all-round efficiency are imposed.

Observations were next directed to the action of the brakes and the value of engine compression for retardation purposes while proceeding from the crest of Purley Way to the Brighton road. The decline also served for a running test for tractive resistance, and when running in 'neutral' the coach showed no signs of undue friction. We were unable to detect anything more audible than the hissing of the tyres, the silent running of the vehicle under normal driving conditions being equally as good. A gentle application of the vacuum hydraulic brakes at 30mph brought the coach to rest with a smooth, progressive action, while the handbrake, designed for use when the coach is in motion — as distinct from a mere parking convenience — served its purpose admirably. After a pause at the Purley traffic lights, the Lancet gathered speed rapidly, and a few seconds later was cruising towards Whyteleafe over part of the route included for suspension testing purposes.

Suspension

Steering the coach over the worst of the familiar surface irregularities at varying speeds, we found the generously proportioned springs fully capable of absorbing severe road shocks without setting up noticeable oscillations. The driving wheels maintained a continuous rolling action whilst propelling the coach smoothly over the rough surface, whilst no shocks or vibrations were transferred from the front wheels to the driver's hands through the steering mechanism. Encouraged by the Lancet's performance thus far, we had no misgivings about the inclusion of an abnormally steep hill in the itinerary, even though the standard back-axle ratio is as high as 5.6 to 1.

In addition to offering a very good test for hill climbing performances, this gradient, which increases to 1 in 5, also permits accurate observations as to the suitability of gear ratios, clutch action, and general ease of vehicle control. Starting the climb on second gear, the Lancet made rapid progress towards the first severe gradient of 1 in 6. Vehicles showing no reserve of power here fail invariably at the summit, but the Lancet responded so promptly to the call for full power as to leave no doubt upon the issue.

After changing down to bottom gear the climb was continued on that ratio, for, although second gear could have been introduced, a change up was hardly worthwhile before the more severe gradient was tackled. As a result, the powerful and smooth running 'Big 4' engine made light work of the easier part of the climb, and when opened out for the 1 in 5 section developed ample power.

On reaching the summit the engine showed no abnormal rise in temperature, and, satisfied on that point, we proceeded towards Upper Warlingham. After passing through the village on top normal gear we introduced the overspeed ratio and depressed the accelerator fully to travel for a short distance at maximum speed. Then the speedometer needle soon passed the 56mph mark, at which speed the coach travelled quite smoothly with great stability and riding comfort. By virtue of its useful reserve of power and performance, the Lancet has a good margin for economical operation at reasonably high cruising speed without extending the engine. In this connection the overspeed gear ratio presents a marked advantage and is well worth the extra cost involved.

The next observed section of the course is at Worms Heath, where varying gradients are encountered representing normal give-and-take main road conditions. Here we quite expected a short spell on third gear at best, but making a fast approach on the overspeed gear the Lancet started at 36mph, the fourth ratio being engaged at 22mph, which took us over the summit at 35mph. Even at the steepest gradient of the series a speed of 19mph was registered on fourth or normal top gear. Once again the 'Big 4' engine revealed the six-cylinder performance claimed by its manufacturers, which can be accepted as being literally true.

A further display of brake performance occurred during the descent of Titsey Hill (1 in 6), when at 30mph a normal application of the footbrake reduced the speed to a walking pace in a few seconds. The pedal was released to allow an increase in speed, and depressed again to be held down hard. This gave the drums and shoes opportunity to warm, a further test at the bottom of the hill proving no appreciable loss in retardation efficiency due to brake temperature. The all-round performance of the Lancet is so good as to occasion difficulty in picking out any outstanding feature, although this particular test emphasised the quality of Dennis brakes.

From Titsey Hill the run was continued through Limpsfield, and thence along the undulating and tortuous road to Westerham, where an easy cruising speed was maintained by liberal use of the overspeed gear. When negotiating the narrow and acute turn from the Square at Westerham into the London road, the useful turning circle and good castoring action of the Lancet's steering gear enabled it to sweep round the corner with plenty of room to spare. After this full-lock manoeuvre the steering wheel was released, whereupon the front wheels straightened up automatically.

Westerham Hill

The four-cylinder engine's capacity for hard work showed up well as we proceeded up the long drag from Westerham to the Pilgrim's Way, where the timed climb of Westerham Hill begins. The long gradient brought us down to third gear, but whereas this test is generally made with a flying start, the Lancet was balked by another vehicle at the crossroads and had to restart on second gear. This ratio served for a speed of 8mph until the first bend on the 1 in 6 part of the hill was approached, the engine pulling strongly all the time on about three-quarters throttle. Later the second ratio was engaged, and the climb was finished at 20mph in third gear, the total time being 3min 26.2sec. Throughout the whole test the Lancet satisfied every requirement as to acceleration and braking efficiency, but in order to present comparative data on these points our usual series of timed checks were taken on a straight level length of road presenting a good surface, the results of which are recorded in the accompanying tables.

The run back to Croydon included many steep hills and difficult descents, which imposed further tests of durability and reliability, but notwithstanding the rigours of the trial the Lancet came through with flying colours. The test certainly revealed the possibilities of a really good four-cylinder petrol coach equipped with a first-class power unit and aided by a five-speed gearbox which certainly makes for better performance and reduced running costs.

Below left: With the driver anxiously peering out of his cab window, a Dennis Lancet ascends Gravelly Hill during another road test. The condition of the road over which the vehicle is running is noteworthy; many roads over which the tests were undertaken during this period lacked a proper surface.

Above: The contemporary information for this Dennis Lancet records, in 1937, that this vehicle was a 'Typical example from the many Dennis coaches commissioned in time for Easter service — a long-wheelbase Lancet owned by Messrs B. Ridley & Son of Erdington, Birmingham'.

Right: The Dennis Lancet demonstrator coach EPD594 is pictured outside the Falkirk premises of Walter Alexander & Sons Ltd during 1936.

Below right: JA2223 was a Dennis Lancet I fitted with ECW 32-seat bodywork delivered new to North Western. It is pictured as No 21 in the fleet of G & B Motor Services of Quarrington Hill, County Durham. *R. C. Davis*

Left: **West Yorkshire Road Car Co No 874 was one of a batch of 18 Dennis Lancet Is delivered in 1936. It was pictured in early 1936, when brand new, on the Stray at Harrogate. The buses were fitted with Eastern Counties 32-seat bodywork.**

Test Results at a Glance

Details of Vehicle

Model:	Dennis 'Lancet' single-decker with 'Big 4' petrol engine
Maker:	Dennis Bros Ltd, Guildford, Surrey
Capacity:	32 seats
Engine:	Make, Dennis. Number of cylinders, 4. Valves, overhead. Bore, 120mm. Stroke, 150mm. Total volume, 6,786cc. Max power, 97bhp at 2,000rpm. RAC rating, 35.7
Transmission:	Type of clutch, dry two-plate. Frictional area, 429sq in. Type of gears, double contact. Number of gears, 5. Form of control, forward
Gear Ratios:	First, 5.19 to 1; second, 2.94 to 1; third, 1.55 to 1; fourth, 1 to 1; overspeed, 0.69 to 1.
Brakes:	Drum diameter (front) 17in (rear) 17in. Total brake area, 485sq in. Method of operation, footbrake acts on front and rear wheels, hydraulically-operated pedal pressure multiplied by vacuum servo; handbrake operates on rear wheels
Wheelbase:	17ft 5in
Body Length:	24ft
Licensing Weight:	32-seater
Annual Tax:	£57 12s (£57.60)
Type of Bodywork:	Coach, Sunsaloon type
Bodymaker:	Dennis Bros
Chassis Price:	£700; 5-speed gearbox £35 extra; self-starter £25 extra
Body Price:	£695

Test Results

Description and Length of Route:	*Modern Transport* Southern Route, 30 miles, hilly and tortuous
Weather:	Fine and cold
Route Conditions:	Good
Gross Weight:	9 tons
Pay Load:	2 tons
Average Speed:	26.4mph
Number of Stops:	Six incidental to special tests
Fuel Consumption:	8mpg
Fuel Used:	No 3 Commercial spirit
Gross Ton mpg:	72
Pay Load Ton mpg:	16
Maximum Gradient Climbed:	1 in 5
Length:	150yd
Turning Circles:	Right lock 62ft; left lock, 62ft
Adjustments During Test:	None
Acceleration:	From 0-30mph, top gear only: 21.2sec From 0-30mph, through all gears: 18sec From 10-30mph, top gear only: 16sec
Braking:	From 30mph to rest, footbrake: 3sec From 30mph to rest, handbrake: 7sec From 30mph to rest, both brakes: 2.8sec
Estimated Maximum Speed:	58mph

—— AEC Regal Oil-Engined Chassis ——

The AEC Regal chassis submitted recently for test under new conditions obtaining in connection with our revised trial arrangements is one of the latest type equipped with the new Comet Mark III oil engine. Details of the new power unit have already been described, but in passing we may offer a few comparisons of its capacity with that of the engine employed formerly. The bore and stroke of 105mm and 146mm, as compared with 100mm and 130mm, has increased the total swept volume to 7,700 cu cm, and the maximum output from 95bhp to 125bhp at 2,400rpm, though actually the engine governor is set normally to limit the speed to 2,000rpm in the interests of fuel economy.

Though generally cleaned up in detail, the chassis shows no apparent departure from previous models, all units of which have stood the test of time. The chassis, which had only covered 150 miles previous to our road test, was driven from the AEC factory at Southall and carried test weights representing 34 passengers and a full bodywork allowance. Inclement weather prevailed while the test was in progress.

Good Accessibility

From the viewpoint of mechanical maintenance, the chassis as a whole is of exceptionally clean design with good accessibility for all units as an outstanding feature of the lay-out. Careful study of bus and coach operation from the aspects of safety and ease of driving is evidenced in the arrangement of the controls, the convenient grouping of the switches in a unit at the driver's right hand, and a really comfortable position at the wheel. More quiet than its predecessors, particularly at idling speeds, the new Comet Mark III oil engine is a quick starter and accelerates willingly under load. AEC worm and nut steering, now standardised on all the company's passenger types, provides a light action and a lower ratio than formerly to reduce the physical effort on the part of the driver.

The single-plate clutch with the generous area of 360sq in acts under low unit pressure and only requires slight effort to ensure quiet and accurate gear engagement, either up or down, aided by a conveniently located ball-ended selector lever. Servo-assisted Lockheed brakes operate in 17in diameter drums giving a total braking area of 504sq in, and the handbrake lever is situated in a good position for use when the vehicle is in motion, thus permitting its ready use for checking the speed without excessive use of the footbrake, which is a great convenience for the driver on long journeys.

Below: **According to the contemporary press statement dated 8 September 1937 it was the performance of an AEC Reliance, acquired in 1928 and seen on the right next to the four AEC Regent double-deckers, that prompted A. Mayne & Sons Ltd of Manchester to concentrate on the AEC marque. Closest to the camera are five AEC Regals acquired by the company which were used primarily on the route to Manchester. The double-deckers were used on a route in Manchester where, the press statement continues, the company is the last independent operator.**

Hill Climbing Performance

Leaving the starting point at Godstone Green for a nonstop run over the 30 miles route, we travelled for some distance along the main road to observe the general behaviour of the chassis and to familiarise ourselves with the controls before attempting to record any performance results. The new Comet engine certainly revealed great possibilities, while the chassis as a whole proved easy and agreeable to handle, despite the indifferent weather conditions.

By the time the fork leading to Tilburstow Hill was reached we were quite at home with the model and started to tackle the long gradient with confidence.

Here the chassis underwent a good test for engine power and the suitability of its gear ratios for service in hilly districts. Passing the first timing point on top gear at 30mph, the Regal continued until the rising gradient necessitated the use of third gear, the vehicle then continuing easily towards the steepest part of the ascent until just before reaching the 1 in 6 portion, when second gear was introduced. From that point to the summit some 200yd ahead a speed of 15mph was maintained, and the climb was completed in 2min 48.4sec.

Immediately after this first climb we found opportunity for testing the brakes under very exacting conditions on a descent of 200ft in the next mile. For part of the distance a speed of 30mph was maintained with the footbrake in partial action to observe the subsequent brake action under the influence of abnormal drum temperature. Stopping tests, checked against a stop-watch, produced the results shown, with acceleration figures, in the accompanying table, the

Left: **This 130hp oil-engined AEC Regal was supplied for working the Grey-Green services of George Ewer & Co Ltd in late 1933.**

Left: **Originally constructed in 1931, this Southend Corporation AEC Regal was pictured at the Corporation's main depot, London Road, in May 1963. No 203 was fitted from new with an English Electric body, but this was later rebuilt by Southend itself. *G. R. Mills***

retardation in all cases being fully progressive and productive of no wheel skids or deviations from a true course. In obtaining these figures very little effort was required in applying the foot or handbrakes, the combined vacuum and hydraulic method of operation satisfying all test requirements in full. The usual acceleration tests took place on a level stretch of main road near Blindley Heath, where the Regal was first stopped by releasing the clutch with the selector lever still in top gear position. The engine was then accelerated to its maximum speed, when, by allowing the clutch to engage gradually, the chassis moved away without any snatch or irregularity in the transmission until a speed of 30mph was reached.

Remarkable responsiveness by the engine to the fuel pump control pedal assisted the quick gear changing necessary to achieve a speed of 30mph from a standing start, when using the four gears progressively, in 27.2sec. The result suggests the ability of this model to maintain close bus

schedules in town work involving numerous stops and restarts. The third acceleration test from 10 to 30mph on top gear showed the engine capable of exerting adequate torque at low speed and pulling evenly under very heavy load. All three acceleration tests imposed severe stresses upon the engine and transmission alike, but nothing occurred to reveal lack of mechanical perfection in any portion of the chassis.

Behaviour when Cruising

The value of increased power output had a great influence on the smooth running of the chassis at normal cruising speeds, which also benefited from the

Right: Captured at Brora during a demonstration run for Highland Transport Co Ltd in early 1933, this diesel-engined AEC Regal was running over the Inverness-Wick route. Standing on the right is the company's General Manager, Mr Fowkes, and in the middle is the Traffic Manager, Mr Hutchinson. All are well-protected against the cold of the Scottish winter.

Right: Pictured at MacBrayne's Glasgow depot during World War 2, this AEC Regal with Park Royal bodywork was delivered to the Scottish operator in 1939. Originally numbered 108, the coach was renumbered 5 in 1942 and was eventually withdrawn in 1953.

flexibility of the engine mountings, the quiet operation of the gears, and a well-balanced transmission, including the underslung worm final drive. Wide variations in road speed were possible on top gear, thanks to the flexibility of the engine, and many of the gradients between Felbridge and Horley were surmounted with ample power in reserve on the direct drive. Here again we noticed that the new Comet engine performs with commendable silence, particularly if one regulates the foot pressure on the accelerator pedal to find the critical engine speed to ensure the greatest silence whilst cruising at the maximum legal speed on top gear.

Ease of Manoeuvre

The winding route covered while the fuel consumption test was in progress emphasised all the qualities in the Regal chassis design which make for ease and safe manoeuvre under all driving conditions. Gear changing requires the minimum of effort, and the brakes respond instantly to light pressure on the pedal. Even when encountering thick traffic on the steep main road through Redhill there was no difficulty in manoeuvring the chassis where road space was greatly restricted by the presence of other vehicles moving in both directions.

Maximum Performance Tests

Soon after leaving Redhill via the steep ascent of Redstone Hill, we entered the final section of the test route, where road and gradient conditions were abnormally severe. The capacity of the latest Regal chassis for really hard work was demonstrated by a faultless ascent on bottom gear of White Hill, where a maximum gradient of 1 in 4 is encountered at the end of a gruelling climb of one mile in length. Here the engine showed no hesitation and pulled the fully-laden chassis in highly commendable style.

Update

The AEC Regal (type 662) firest appeared in 1929 as a single-deck companion to the double-deck AEC Regent launched earlier the same year. The model was initially petrol-engined (with a 6.1litre engine), but a diesel version first appeared in 1931 (using a 8.8litre engine) Diesel-engined models were classified O662. A third option appeared in 1934 with the availability of a 7.7litre engine; this was the version featured in the road test. The Gardner 6LW was provided as an additional option in 1935. Production ceased in 1940; a handful of the several thousand produced have survived into preservation

Test Results at a Glance

Details of Vehicle		Test Results	
Model:	AEC Regal Type 0662	Description and	
Maker:	AEC Ltd, Southall	Length of Route:	Modern Transport New Southern Route, 30 miles, varied contours and conditions
Capacity:	34 passengers		
Engine:	Make, AEC. Number of cylinders, 6. Valves, overhead. Bore,105mm. Stroke, 146mm. Total volume, 7,700cc. Maximum power, 125bhp at 2,400rpm. RAC rating, 41	Weather:	Wet and windy
		Route Conditions:	Indifferent
		Gross Weight:	8ton 5cwt
		Pay Load:	Equivalent to 34 passengers
Transmission	Type of clutch, single plate. Frictional area, 360sq in. Type of gears, spur. Number of gears, 4 and reverse. Form of control, normal. Cardan shaft, AEC. Final drive, underslung worm with fully floating axle. Final ratio, (standard) 5.5 to 1, (alternative) 5.75 to 1 and 6.5 to 1. Model tested was fitted with 5.75 to 1 ratio	Average Speed:	23mph
		Number of Stops:	Six incidental to special tests
		Fuel Consumption:	10mpg
		Fuel Used:	Shell-Mex Diesoleum
		Maximum Gradient	
		Climbed:	1 in 4
		Length:	100yd
		Turning Circles:	Right lock, 60ft. Left lock, 60ft
		Adjustments	
		During Test:	None
Gear Ratios:	First, 4.38 to 1; second, 2.69 to 1; third, 1.59 to 1; fourth, direct. Auxiliary ratio, none	Acceleration:	From 0-30mph, top gear only: 36.4sec From 0-30mph, through all gears: 27.2sec From 10-30mph, top gear only: 24.4sec
Brakes:	Drum diameter, (front) 17in (rear) 17in. Total brake area, 504sq in. Method of operation: internal expanding servo-assisted Lockheed. Handbrake for rear wheels	Braking:	From 30mph to rest, footbrake: 3.4sec From 30mph to rest, handbrake: 5.2sec From 30mph to rest, both brakes: 3.4sec
Wheelbase:	17ft 6in		
Licensing Weight:	4ton 3cwt 2lb		
Chassis Price:	£1,250	Estimated Maximum	
Body Space:	23ft 1in. Capacity up to 37 seats	Speed:	40mph

20 June 1947
——Foden Single-Deck Chassis——

It was with considerable interest that I accepted the invitation of Fodens Ltd, of Sandbach, Cheshire, to carry out a road test of one of their new single-deck vehicles early in June. This vehicle, it will be remembered, was first announced by the company in 1945, and a description of it appeared in our issue of 14 September in that year. Since that date the company has carried out various small modifications to the chassis and recently several of the vehicles have been put into service. So far, out of some 50 ordered, over 20 have been delivered and are operating with very good results.

When I carried out the road test on the single-deck chassis on 3 June, it happened that the date coincided with the hottest day of the year so far, when temperatures exceeded 90° Fahrenheit. While this was very pleasant from the personal aspect, it did mean that the sun, by reducing the roads to sheets of molten tar, made things very difficult for obtaining consistent performance readings, particularly when carrying out the brake tests. Despite this, as will be seen from the tables appearing later in this article, good figures were obtained.

After fitting the Tapley brake and performance meters, checking the laden weight of the chassis, and making sure that tyre pressures were up to standard, I had the fuel tank completely filled to the top of the filler, as it had been decided to take the fuel consumption figures over the complete test route. Incidentally, as I did not know the country round Sandbach particularly well, I had asked Fodens to arrange a route for me capable of demonstrating the vehicle's possibilities. Their faith in the chassis was

Below: **The hill test was carried out climbing Dane in Shaw Hill after leaving Congleton. The chassis is caught passing under the ex-North Staffordshire line from Congleton via Biddulph to Stoke.**

performance meter. These are shown in the chart below and in each case the figures were obtained making late gear changes, but even so, the Gardner 6LW engine kept the vehicle speed at a minimum of 7mph.

The route continued over Cloud End, around through Bosley and Rushton, then back over Cloud End again, through Congleton, Somerford and so on to Holmes Chapel. Here lunch was taken at the 'Good Companions', and the carpark there proved to be an ideal spot for checking the vehicle's turning circles. On right lock the figure obtained was 62ft 8in and on left lock 62ft. After leaving Holmes Chapel, a stretch of level road was at last found between there and Brereton. By this time, however, the recently tarred roads were in a very soft state, so that the figures taken are probably somewhat lower than I would have obtained in normal circumstances. The tractive resistance figure of 45lb/ton, again obtained on the Tapley meter, proved that the transmission and the vehicle in general was quite free-running, as this figure was undoubtedly increased by the wet tar which could be heard sucking into the tyre treads. Nevertheless, the fact that this was the only level stretch of road meant that the tests had to be continued there.

Firstly, then, I carried out a timed start from rest through all the gears to 30mph and this took 36sec in one direction and 30sec on the return journey. Then followed a rolling acceleration test in top gear from 10mph to 30mph, a test designed to show engine performance for acceleration and maximum power over the lower end of its speed range. The times of 34.2sec and 36sec were therefore very good, as the vehicle had a 4.4 to 1 rear axle ratio.

The road speed acceleration results were next taken, and here again the tarry roads influenced the Tapley figures.

Finally on the same stretch of road, the brake tests were carried out and here the road conditions had a very definite effect on the results as the road surface gave way when the brakes were applied fully, causing considerable skidding to take place. I first of all arranged for the brakes to be applied in such a way that on a complete vehicle any passengers would not have been unduly inconvenienced — in other words they were applied in a perfectly normal manner. At a road speed of 25mph, and with the clutch disengaged, the percentage efficiency was given as 42% on the Tapley brake performance meter. Next the handbrake was applied with the clutch disengaged while the vehicle was travelling at the same speed, and again the result was a figure of 42%. The maximum footbrake operation, again from a speed of 25mph with the clutch released, proved to be very

such that the route they decided on was just about as gruelling as it could have been, including as it did, a switchback journey to Cloud End at the summit of the southernmost tip of the Pennine range.

The first five or six miles of the journey covered a reasonably level route, although the many sharp bends and particularly a near-hairpin bend running into Congleton demonstrated the easy manoeuvrability of the large vehicle. It was in Congleton, too, that a sharp application of the brakes showed their easy responsiveness to quite a light pedal pressure. Here also I used the hill-holder, which is fitted as standard, and found that it was a great help when pulling away.

Leaving Congleton, there is a long pull up Dane Inn Shaw Hill, and this proved admirable for obtaining the hill climbing results. A most satisfactory stop and restart test was carried out on a 1 in 5 gradient, and the maximum pull results were then obtained on the same hill using the Tapley

difficult to obtain as the road surface gave way, so that long skids resulted, and the best figure obtained under these conditions gave an efficiency reading of only 60%. It is worth noting, however, that whilst skidding, the vehicle kept a perfectly straight course and that the pressures on the brake drums were therefore exactly equalised. On the final stage of the trip back to Sandbach, I was able to find one very short stretch of level road that had not been recently tarred, and took the opportunity of trying one further full application of the footbrake, again from a speed of 25mph. This resulted in an efficiency of 71% — a very satisfactory result.

The vehicle performed extremely well throughout the whole of its tests. Its gross weight of 9ton 9cwt 1qtr was over the figure to be expected when in service, but nevertheless, gear changing and steering proved to be quite easy. The four-speed gearbox, with its constant mesh helical gears, was silent in operation. I was also agreeably surprised at the driving comfort; the alloy housing of the steering column and the mounting of the steering wheel damped out all vibration, so that the vehicle was a pleasure to drive. Another feature of interest from the driver's point of view was the light pedal operation for both footbrake and clutch. The footbrake is assisted by a simply-operated oil booster and the powerful two-leading show brakes gave very good results. The engine — the well-known Gardner 6LW direct injection model developing 102bhp at 1,700rpm — did all that was asked of it and it was a pleasure to drive along at 45mph with the feeling that the vehicle could go on all day like that if necessary.

The patented method of cruciform cross-bracing adopted by Fodens Ltd provides a means of withstanding the heaviest torsional stresses, and the three-point patented flexible engine suspension and rubber insulated centre propeller shaft mounting both combine to cut down chassis vibration very considerably.

On returning to the Foden works at Sandbach, the amount of fuel used on the 38 miles run was carefully checked by adding fuel to the tank until the level was back to its original state. This showed that over the whole run, which included all the performance tests, 3.3125gal had been used, giving a fuel consumption figure of 11.47mpg under very arduous conditions.

The results obtained, considering the conditions under which they were taken, show that the vehicle is satisfactory in all respects and its performance, coupled with unorthodox but very pleasant appearance and easy accessibility for maintenance, should put it well to the fore in the field of coach operations.

Update

The Foden PVSC single-deck first appeared in 1946, following on from the PVD double-deck model that had been launched the previous year. The single-deck chassis was offered with a choice of Gardner 5LW (the PVSC5) or 6LW (the PVSC6) engine. A third engine option, the two-stroked Foden FD6, was introduced in 1948. Production of the type ceased in 1956.

Right: With the observer carefully watching over his shoulder, the driver eases the Foden around the test run. The weights, added to the chassis to simulate a full body and passenger load, are clearly visible.

Maximum Pull on Test Hill			Road Speed Acceleration			
Gear	Pull lb/ton	Gradient	Gear	Pull lb/ton	Changed gear at	Ft/sec
Fourth	55	1 in 15	First	200	9mph	2.9
Third	150	1 in 14	Second	150	15mph	2.2
Second	220	1 in 10	Third	120	25mph	1.7
First	360	1 in 6	Fourth	70	—	1.0

—Daimler CVD6 Single-Deck Chassis—

On 13 March 1948 members of the Omnibus Society inspected the *Modern Transport* test route. By courtesy of Transport Vehicles (Daimler) Ltd, the party was able to traverse this rigorous course on a Daimler CVD6 coach chassis fitted with a 35-seat Willowbrook service bus body. The particular chassis concerned has a high back axle ratio specially suited to economical running at the legal limit on long coach journeys and its performance on the steep pitches of the North Downs was therefore specially meritorious. It is a rare occasion when a human load is available for the purposes of performing a road test with a passenger chassis, but the personnel concerned on this occasion were specially welcome as they provided a very useful and critical test load. It was a demonstration, too, of the procedure involved in the tests and the several innovations and deviations which have lately been introduced for the better testing of vehicle performance. With *Modern Transport* and Daimler staff the total number of passengers was 33.

As the time of the demonstration to the Omnibus Society was limited, all the observed tests were completed two days earlier over the same route and we were able, therefore, both to form our own opinions from driving the vehicle and to ascertain the reaction of the passengers after enduring the rigours of the difficult route. The load on the first occasion comprised test weights to make a total of 9ton 10cwt gross, nearly that of a double-decker, while on the second trip the load was estimated at 8ton 16cwt, so that some interesting comparisons were possible between the two trips.

Smooth Getaway

After weighing the laden bus at Croydon Gasworks, we returned to Croydon Airport for the start of the test. We were blessed with fine weather on both days and the Daimler made a smooth getaway in first gear each time. A quick acceleration in each of the three ratios brought us to the statutory speed, whereafter we eased our foot from the accelerator pedal to keep within the speed limit. It was not until half-way up Purley Way that the speed commenced to slacken and for a while we thought that we should be able to reach the top of the ascent in that gear. However, as our speed was slowly dropping to 20mph, we considered at this stage that overstraining of the engine was inadvisable and the short distance to the top was completed in third gear at

25mph. On the later run with the party, although the load was not quite as heavy, the speeds and gears coincided with the first test.

This Daimler bus had completed approximately 50,000 miles on demonstrations to operators in this country and the necessity for the free-running test hardly arose, but our interest in the quiet running vehicle caused us to engage neutral for a short distance to listen for transmission and body noise. Both were consciously absent. We had been informed already by Mr T. W. Wood, of the Daimler Sales Department, who accompanied us on both tests, that, other than normal maintenance work, no adjustments had been made to the bus since its completion at the Coventry works.

The road from Purley to Caterham requires normal running procedure to be adopted and does not call for any unusual driving tactics, such as the use of indirect gears or rapid manoeuvring of the steering. It does, however, provide a chance to observe the vehicle's handling characteristics in light traffic. In this matter the Daimler created a very favourable impression with regard to ease of control, for on one occasion when a service bus made a rapid stop ahead of us, we braked smoothly, engaged a lower gear and were

soon accelerating round the bus — four operations completed without effort in a matter of seconds.

Passing through Caterham we retained top gear to negotiate safely the busy town at a speed of about 23mph, and turned back on the bypass, where we reached a speed of over 40mph on the spiralling descent to the Warlingham roundabout. Swinging the coach from one side of the carriageway to the other we hoped to set up a rather unsteady motion in the interior of the coach. This did not materialise, for although we had zigzagged four times, as we straightened up the steering of the bus became perfectly steady immediately. There had been no unpleasant sensation during this test and the general opinion of the passengers was that they had felt very comfortable.

Left: Dating from 1949, West Riding No 341 was a Daimler CVD6 fitted with a Willowbrook body that was originally new to the Bullock fleet and which passed to West Riding when Bullock was taken over. It was photographed in the West Riding coach livery prior to being repainted in the service bus livery. Ironically, the aged Daimler outlasted the new AEC Reliance visible on the right. *Paul G. Ogden*

Above right: Pictured in Balance Street, Uttoxeter, during July 1956, this Daimler CVD6 with Burlingham body, No SN374, was in service with PMT. Route numbers, including this Stafford-based one, were almost completely recast in February 1958. *A. Moyes*

Right: One Burwell & District Daimler CVD6 was this Heaver-bodied example, MCE201, that was new in February 1954. The vehicle provided accommodation for 35 seated passengers. *G. R. Mills*

Stop and Restart on 1 in 6

Here, at the Warlingham roundabout, the more severe section of our test route commences. In view of the rear axle ratio of 4.66 to 1 we went direct to Bug Hill, which ascends at 1 in 6. Here the Daimler bus made an easy climb in first gear and we were also able to make a stop and restart on the steepest section of the hill. We were quite confident of the Daimler achieving this severe test and were pleased to think that 33 others could share our confidence in the chassis.

A few miles farther on we came to Worms Heath which was approached at 30mph in top gear; the gradient proved a little too severe for the vehicle in this gear and third was engaged to finish the climb at a speed ranging from 20-25mph. We reintroduced top gear quickly to prepare for the maximum speed

test along the wide stretch of concrete road overlooking the Caterham Valley. The speedometer fitted to this model had a top register figure of 40mph and when the needle reached this point we were travelling fast and still accelerating and our final estimate of the speed was about 46mph. Over the succeeding upgrade to the top of Titsey Hill our speed was maintained at 38mph.

No Brake Fade on Heating

Descending Titsey Hill (1 in 6), a light pressure on the footbrake, at the notice-board warning drivers to descend in low gear, retarded the vehicle's speed to 8mph, and this speed was maintained to the church, where, with smoke rising from the hot linings, the usual hard application brought us to a standstill, almost too violently for some of the passengers, within 15ft — a sure sign of brake durability.

Taking a bus or coach through Miry Miriam Lane might be regarded by many as a freak, but in this case we had two reasons for doing so: one to show our passengers the more difficult 'colonial' sections of the route and secondly to provide the sensations of travel which are experienced in certain overseas markets for British bus chassis. A short pause was made for photographs and examination of the terrain. Plunging into the water-splash, we engaged second gear in preparation for the extra effort which we thought the engine would have to make to

Above left: Swindon Corporation No 57 was a Daimler CVD6 fitted with a Park Royal centre-entrance body. It was delivered in 1947 and on withdrawal was sold to Nuneaton Borough Council, which fitted it with a public-address system and a replacement radiator from an ex-Birmingham Corporation double-decker. *C. B. Workman*

Left: Dating from 1948, this Burlingham-bodied Daimler CVD6 was fitted with a 33-seat coach body. Numbered D19 in the Alexander (Northern) fleet, the vehicle was one of three Daimler CVD6 single-deckers owner by Alexanders that survived into preservation. *Iain MacGregor*

Right: SHMD No 103 was a Northern Counties-bodied 35-seat Daimler CVD6. *J. J. Holmes*

propel us through the mud and ruts and over the large stones with which the track is strewn. The way in which we lurched, rolled, pitched and tossed made us reconsider our resolution to cover the whole route. This, nevertheless, was difficult to change, for once partially submerged in the mire there is little chance of turning back. We found the pre-selective gear change very helpful over this section of the route, for it was necessary the whole time to keep a firm hold on the steering wheel and at several suitable junctures we were able to introduce third gear. It was a performance that brought much favourable comment from the passengers and on the one occasion when we did manage a quick glance in the saloon of the bus, we saw a sea of happy faces. Our speed throughout this section was between 10 and 15mph.

Absence of Driving Fatigue

We continued through Limpsfield and followed the roundabout route through Crockham Hill, Puddledock and Toys Hill, the vehicle being driven at all speed ranges with the use of all four gears. It was by no means the first time we had driven a vehicle with a fluid flywheel and pre-selective epicyclic gearbox on the road, but it was the first use of this exhausting deviation — so typical of a class of bus route either in city streets or in the country which the professional bus driver classifies as a 'shoulder-breaker' — with a vehicle so equipped. Here it proved its value beyond doubt, for on arrival at Toys Hill, having overcome the most difficult of the byways, no sign of fatigue or physical warmth was noticeable.

Owing to the vehicle's long wheelbase, it may be noted, we had been unable to enter the lane from Puddledock to Horsey Common and Westerham, used for our freight vehicle tests, hence the diversion (not shown in the diagram on page 5) via Toys Hill and Brasted to Westerham.

Returning to the usual route at Westerham we timed the climb of Westerham Hill (1 in 6) from the Pilgrims' Way, at which place we engaged second gear and were driving at a speed of 15mph. In another 50yd, first gear was engaged to finish the climb, including the steepest portion of the hill, at 10mph with a good reserve of engine power. The time to complete the half-mile test was 3min 14sec and on checking the radiator temperature it was observed that the cooling water was still well below overheating point.

The first part of the fuel consumption test follows a stage carriage route to Biggin Hill, where it turns off the main Bromley road to follow some rather narrow and steep unclassified roads to West Wickham, thence by bus routes back to Croydon Airport. We did not make any stops other than for traffic and therefore expected a fairly good fuel consumption. The resultant figure of 15.5mpg is obviously very satisfactory.

Throughout the test we had been impressed by the well-placed controls and good driving position which had contributed so much to the pleasure of our drive. Moreover the Daimler engine was quite unobtrusive, for in spite of the usual diesel engine sound it was reasonably quiet. This fact had also been noticed by those who were travelling inside the bus. As our table reveals, the braking and acceleration were of a high order and were obtained smoothly and without exertion. It had been a very successful test, reflecting much credit on the Daimler company for its excellent chassis and on Willowbrook for the smart and comfortable body. Our passengers, it was interesting to note, shared while riding the favourable opinion we had formed of the machine whilst driving it.

Left: **Pictured on 11 December 1966 in Blackpool, when operating on a Nottingham University Transport Society tour, W. Gash & Son Ltd's No 4 was a 1949-vintage, Burlingham-bodied Daimler CVD6. Accommodation was provided for 35 seated passengers.** *J. R. Denham*

Update

The single-deck Daimler CV series was launched in 1947, one year after the parallel double-deck model. The latter was fitted with a wheelbase of 16ft 3.25in which made it slightly shorter than the single-deck version (17ft 2.5in). Two engine options were available from either Daimler (hence the CVD6) or Gardner (the CVG5). The latter option was only available until 1949, but the Daimler-engined variant continued in production until 1955.

Test Results at a Glance

Details of Vehicle

Model:	Daimler CVD6 single-deck chassis
Maker:	Transport Vehicles (Daimler) Ltd
Capacity:	35 seats
Engine:	Make, Daimler. Number of cylinders, six. Valves, overhead. Bore, 4.5in. Stroke, 5.5in. Total volume, 8.6litres. Maximum power, 100bhp at 1,800rpm. RAC rating, 48.6
Transmission:	Daimler fluid flywheel. Type of gears, pre-selective. Number of gears, four. Form of control, pre-selector mounted on steering column. Cardan shaft, two open tubular. Final drive, underslung worm. Final ratio (standard), 4.67 to 1
Gear Ratios:	First, 4.15 to 1. Second, 2.36 to 1. Third, 1.56 to 1. Fourth, direct
Brakes:	Drum diameter (front), 16.75in. Drum diameter (rear), 16.75in. Total brake area, 597sq in. Method of operation, Lockheed servo-assisted
Wheelbase:	17ft 2.5in
Body Length:	22ft 6in
Type of Bodywork:	Single-deck bus
Bodymaker:	Willowbrook Ltd, Loughborough

Test Results

Description and Length of Route:	*Modern Transport* southern test route through Surrey and Kent, 44 miles
Weather:	Fine and dry
Route Conditions:	Very good
Gross Weight:	9ton 10cwt
Pay Load:	2ton 15cwt or 44 passengers (included nine standing)
Average Speed:	22mph
Number of Stops:	Five
Fuel Consumption:	15.5mpg
Gross Ton mpg:	107.25
Passenger mpg:	682
Maximum Gradient Climbed:	1 in 4.25
Length:	0.5 mile
Turning Circles:	Right lock, 66ft. Left lock, 66ft
Adjustments During Test:	None
Acceleration:	From 0-30mph, through all gears: 28.5sec. From 10-30mph, top gear only: 35.5sec
Braking:	From 30mph to rest, footbrake: 40ft. From 20mph to rest, handbrake: 17ft
Estimated Maximum Speed:	46mph

Bristol K6B

When an operator designs and manufactures his own passenger chassis it is pretty certain that the product will be capable of giving a reliable service at low running cost with a sound economy of maintenance. This is the case with the Bristol range of passenger vehicles built by the manufacturing side of the Bristol Tramways & Carriage Co Ltd, which has been operating a large fleet of buses. These are mostly the product of its own works at Brislington, Bristol, and particular attention has been paid, therefore, by the designers to the object of obtaining an operating mileage period between major overhauls of from 100,000 to 120,000 miles. How successful it has been needs no better substantiation than the appearance of many of the latest Bristol K and L-type chassis in service with the latest operators in this country. The latters' enthusiasm for this make was due in no small measure to the simple design of the units incorporated in a conventional lay-out. In fact there are no frills! A recent test of the K6B double-deck chassis on our route provided convincing proof that this principle of simple lay-out, robust construction and an economical power unit was well founded.

When the vehicle arrived at Croydon Airport we made a quick observation of its various features and noted that it was equipped with the latest Bristol AVW-type diesel engine. This engine is a six-cylinder direct injection unit, of 8.25litres capacity, developing 100bhp at 1,700rpm and a torque of 337lb/ft at 1,200rpm. The maximum bmep is 102lb/sq in. A particularly clean appearance has been achieved by the designers whilst at the same time incorporating a notable degree of accessibility. In this latter respect the auxiliaries are worthy of special mention, as an independent drive has been adopted for the CAV fuel injection pump, the CAV or Simms dynamo and the Clayton-Dewandre exhauster and water pump. The monobloc cylinders are fitted with dry liners and are surmounted by two-piece

interchangeable cylinder heads which include both the inlet and exhaust valve ports placed on the nearside. Bristol-patented separate and detachable air intake chokes are fitted, and a copper sleeve is inserted for cooling the injectors. The test load consisted of five one-ton blocks, and in addition there was an observer's cab. The axle loadings were 4ton 19cwt 3qtr front and 6ton 3cwt at the rear.

A Good Start

From force of habit we engaged second gear to start from Croydon when first would have been more suitable, and although we had a maximum load — this was very obvious from the clutch take-up and the torque reaction of the flexibly-mounted engine — we had soon accelerated enough to change into third gear, followed in a short time by top gear. We were now travelling at 20mph, and would have maintained this speed to the top of Purley Way if our road had not been obstructed by some heavy lorries making a slow ascent of the hill. To pass these we re-engaged third speed.

Already the simple lay-out of the controls in the cab had made us feel quite at home, and the first impressions of the Bristol chassis assured us that the remainder of the test could be viewed with confidence. Listening intently as we glided in neutral to the Purley traffic lights, we were immediately impressed by the absence of engine noise when it was idling. Several times later in the test when making traffic stops the horrible thought that our engine had stalled was proved to be a deception by a touch of the accelerator pedal.

Right: **Thames Valley No 469 is seen in Reading on 7 May 1949. This Bristol K6B was new in 1947 and was one of the first K6Bs acquired by Thames Valley and was fitted with an ECW 55-seat body.** *V. C. Jones*

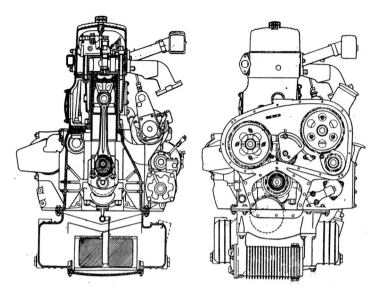

will have no difficulty in maintaining a fast scheduled service under equally or even more difficult conditions.

Brake Fade Negligible

Brake temperature and fade tests were performed over the descent of Titsey Hill, where a controlled speed of 8-10mph was undertaken by a steady application of the footbrake. To overcome the braking effect of the engine compression the clutch was temporarily disengaged. At Titsey Church the speed of the vehicle was momentarily increased to 18mph, then an emergency stop was attempted which brought us to rest within approximately 50ft. On examination the brake drums did not appear to have warmed up excessively even after this gruelling half-mile application.

Bad surface conditions prevailed in Miry Miriam Lane which caused considerable rear wheel spring and restricted our speed to about 10mph in second gear, thereby preventing us from providing the suspension with its usual bouncing. However, the potholes and ruts remained to give the steering and springs some severe jolts. The observer's cab amidships obstructed a complete view of the rear part of the chassis, but the section we could see retained its rigidity. Such a robust frame with its deep-section side-members and tubular cross-members could withstand any amount of distortion. In its centre portion there is a maximum depth of 11in. Turning into the Limpsfield lane, the sharp corner was negotiated comfortably in one move by a full lock of the steering.

Passing through Limpsfield, we made a slick change into third gear well in advance of turning into the A25 road; however, this gear was not low enough to master this short, sharp incline, and second gear was engaged. The undulating nature of the road across Limpsfield Common, where a rise of 200ft is covered in approximately two miles to Crockham Hill, showed that the Bristol engine had a good flexibility in top gear. In this distance speeds ranged from 16mph to 30mph, and several times the engine exhibited its high torque and low speeds.

Hill Climb and Fuel Consumption

Following our route through Crockham Hill, we

Along the Caterham Valley we cruised at a speed of 30mph for a considerable number of miles. Sections of this road have rather bad surfaces, and we felt that the front suspension seemed a little harsh; this may be accounted for by the disposition of the test load, two ton weights being placed directly behind the bulkhead and increasing the percentage of the load on the front axle. This did not affect the steering, however, which is designed to eliminate interference due to variations of spring loading and has the latest Marles double roller type steering box. It proved exceptionally light in the circumstances.

Effortless Gear Change

After this demonstration of good running over a main service bus route we departed from our routine test practice of climbing the Succombs test hill and deviated by way of Bug Hill, where a satisfactory stop and restart was made on its 1 in 6 gradient. Continuing through Warlingham we approached Worms Heath at 30mph, and here we found it necessary to use third gear. This engagement of the third gear from top could be completed so harmoniously — it is a smooth combination of rapid engine pick-up and constant mesh gears engaged by sliding dogs — that labouring in top gear would never be contemplated.

The maximum speed of this model when the engine governor cut in at 1,700rpm was 34.5mph. This speed may appear low for a modern passenger chassis, but when it is considered that we kept the speedometer needle at this figure as far as the top of Titsey Hill, which included a steadily rising road for a good part of the distance, it is obvious that, disregarding legal speed limits, a vehicle with a gross weight of over 11 tons that is going to maintain a consistently high speed under heavy load and severe road conditions

purposely avoided Puddledock and continued direct to Westerham, thereby missing some of the more strenuous corners. The part of the road covered still meant active driving with a quick succession of gear changes followed by smart rotation of the steering wheel, throughout which it confirmed our opinion of its good controllability. The driver's cab, we noted, was very simply planned, with the change speed lever on the left and a pull-on handbrake lever on the right; the three control pedals were also well positioned. A timed climb was then made of Westerham Hill from a standing start at the Pilgrim's Way. We had no difficulty in taking the temperatures of the assemblies because everything is so accessible, and the following were recorded: radiator, 179° Fahrenheit; engine lubricant, 159°F; and rear axle, 145°F.

Starting in second gear, our speed fell away as the gradient increased, and within 50yd we had engaged first gear. We finished the climb in this gear; the engine was now running at governed speed to give the fastest possible time with a maximum road speed of 6mph. It resulted in a time of 4min 30sec for the half-mile distance. Temperatures were again taken and recorded as follows: radiator, 181°F; engine lubricant, 169°F; and rear axle, 165°F. This hill (maximum 1 in 6) is, of course, climbed half-hourly by a double-deck bus.

A fuel consumption test was completed during the return to Croydon. Traffic conditions were light, and the course is of a very give-and-take nature, so that an average result is returned. It was over these roads,

served by regular bus routes, that the Bristol chassis was really a pleasure to drive. Its quick acceleration, sure braking and light control made it easy to manoeuvre amongst the traffic. The driving position gave a good view of the road ahead and at all times one could make a close limit judgement of gaps in the traffic. Next we took the Bristol to Mitcham Common for the brake and acceleration tests, the results of which are shown in the table.

The Bristol test-driver who accompanied us was a brawny young man who put all he could exert into

Right: **Still resplendent despite being 19 years old in 1968, this Bristol K6B of Hants & Dorset, No 1230, was pictured in retirement in Godalming having been secured for preservation.** *David Fereday Glenn*

this brake test, but after three attempts we attained an average stopping distance of 53ft. A conventional triple vacuum servo system is employed, of Clayton-Dewandre manufacture, in conjunction with an efficient Bristol design of linkage and shoe equipment. Continual locking of the nearside rear wheel, however, did not help the result; anyway, a 60% brake efficiency is still very good.

In conclusion, we can only repeat that the Bristol provided an example of how a modern vehicle incorporating such a simple lay-out still proves very successful. It is the type of machine in which every operator can have the utmost confidence.

Update

The original Bristol K-type was introduced in 1937 and by the time that production was suspended in 1942, more than 840 had been constructed. Production resumed in 1944 with either Gardner (K5G) or AEC (K5A) engines. The Bristol-engined version — the K6B — as described in the road test appeared in 1948, the year after the six-cylinder Gardner version (K6G) was launched. Production of the model ceased in 1950, by which time almost 2,000 had been manufactured. It was replaced by the longer and wider (KS and KSW respectively) which continued in production until 1957, by when more than 4,000 had been built.

Left: **Delivered originally in 1949 as West Yorkshire No 751, this Bristol K6B was converted for use as a double-deck coach in 1951, reverting to standard bus use in late 1953. When new it was fitted with an ECW 55-seat body, with seating capacity reduced to 41 during its period of use as a coach. It reverted to being a 55-seat vehicle in 1953. It became No DB23 on the renumbering of the West Yorkshire fleet in April 1954.** *R. F. Mack*

Test Results at a Glance		**Test Results**	
Details of Vehicle		Description and	
Model:	Bristol K6B double-deck chassis	*Length of Route:*	*Modern Transport* Southern Route, 36 miles
Maker:	Bristol Tramways & Carriage Co	*Weather:*	Fair periods
Capacity:	56	*Route Conditions:*	Good
Engine:	Bristol. Number of cylinders, six. Valves, overhead. Bore, 110mm. Stroke, 143mm. Total volume, 8.25litre. Maximum power, 100bhp at 1,700rpm. RAC rating, 45hp	*Gross Weight:*	11ton 3cwt
		Pay Load:	Equivalent to 56 passengers
		Average Speed:	21.5mph
		Number of Stops:	Eight
		Fuel Consumption:	12.7mpg
		Gross Ton mpg:	141.6
		Passenger mpg:	711.2
Transmission:	Type of clutch, single dry plate. Frictional area, 226.9sq in. Type of gears, spun with constant mesh for third. Number of gears, four and a reverse. Form of control, remote. Cardan shaft, two open tubular. Final drive, underslung worm. Final ratio (standard), 5.75 to 1; (alternative), 5.4 to 1, 6.0 to 1 or 6.5 to 1	*Maximum Gradient*	
		Climbed:	1 in 6
		Length:	Five miles
		Turning Circles:	Right lock, 59ft. Left lock, 59ft
		Adjustments	
		During Test:	None
		Acceleration:	From 0-30mph, top gear only: 32.5sec
Gear Ratios:	First: 4.74 to 1; second, 2.74 to 1; third, 1.66 to 1; fourth, direct; reverse, 5.82 to 1		From 0-30mph, through all gears: 15.5sec
			From 10-30mph, top gear only: 26sec
Brakes:	Drum diameter (front), 17in; width, 3.5in. Drum diameter (rear), 17.5in; width, 7.5in. Total brake area, 605sq in. Method of operation, triple vacuum servo	*Braking:*	From 20mph to rest, footbrake: 29.5ft
			From 30mph to rest, footbrake: 53ft
		Estimated Maximum	
Wheelbase:	16ft 3in	*Speed:*	34.5mph
Overall Length:	26ft		

10 December 1948
-Daimler CD650 Double-Deck Chassis-

Under whatever circumstances it may be made, a visit to the Daimler company's works at Coventry is always interesting, but when it concerns the first press road test of a new Daimler passenger model, the occasion may well assume historical importance in the passenger transport industry.

Many years ago when I conducted the first press trip of a Daimler bus chassis equipped with fluid transmission, its performance inspired many remarks to the effect that 'I have at last driven the perfect bus'. Now, as the following report suggests, the company's latest CD650 double-decker chassis, shown for the first time at the Commercial Vehicle Exhibition in London, is a masterpiece in heavy automobile engineering which proves that its producers have now rendered perfection still more perfect.

Before describing details of CD650 performance as revealed by a highly critical road test it is worthy of special mention that, having evolved a highly advanced passenger chassis and satisfied themselves on its general behaviour, Daimler have left nothing to chance in presenting the model for testing in truly trustworthy condition.

For this I think full credit must be given to Mr R. S. Crouch, Head of the Experimental Road Test Department, who is responsible for designing the test equipment. Behind the driver's seat is comfortable accommodation for two observers provided with Tapley performance and brake testing meters, a split-second stop clock, a Zenith fuel consumption tester, water temperature and oil pressure gauges as well as a conveniently arranged ladder for easy access to the observer's department.

I am told, too, that test preparations include experimental arrangements of the load to ensure its accurate distribution to represent actual service loading of a bus under normal working conditions.

Thus prepared for the first press test of the model, Mr R. S. 'Bob' Crouch took the wheel at 10am on the morning of 3 December 1948 at the Radford Works, Coventry. For the first part of the journey I occupied the observer's seat to watch the instruments in order to record the principal items of measured performance.

Below: **The Daimler CD650 chassis is seen outside the Daimler Works, Radford, Coventry prior to a road test on 1 December 1948.**

Above: **During the road test of 1 December 1948 the chassis is seen on Stoneleigh Hill, where a stop and restart test was undertaken on the 1 in 10 gradient.**

In accordance with long established procedure, the first test to be made was one for tractive resistance to make sure that all-round performance was in no way marred by undue friction in any part of the chassis mechanism. As was to be expected from Daimler standards of workmanship, the chassis ran with characteristically free action, which produced the low Tapley tractive resistance of 35lb/ton when allowed to coast at 20mph.

Powered by the new Daimler 10.6litre, six-cylinder direct injection oil engine, supported by three-point axial suspension, the chassis glided smoothly through congested traffic in Coventry as we made for the London road on the way to Stoneleigh Hill, where a long gradient with a maximum incline of 1 in 10 afforded good opportunities of checking pull through the various gear ratios, ease of restarting from rest and braking results.

The hill was approached in top gear at a speed of 30mph, the climb being continued on direct drive until full engine torque was exerted. Then with a flick of the pre-selector lever and a touch of the pedal controlling the hydraulic gear change, the third speed epicyclic gear train came into immediate action and at that precise instant the Tapley meter recorded a top-gear pull of no less than 80lb/ton. Under similar

conditions, the engine produced pulls of 180 and 240lb/ton for third and second speeds respectively. The gradient was not sufficiently steep to give maximum pull on the lowest ratio, the reading of 350lb/ton accorded at the steepest part of the climb being obtained while the engine was running at well below its maximum power output. Two further ascents were made of Stoneleigh Hill to verify the results, when these figures agreed exactly with those stated above. Any doubts I may have had concerning the action of the fluid flywheel under full stress were dispelled for good and all as the chassis made a faultless restart on the 1 in 10 gradient, which, I am sure, could have been much steeper without producing a vestige of slip.

I am told that the open-circuit fluid flywheel, as fitted to all Daimler chassis, has a lag of rather less than 2% between its driving and driven members at ordinary engine speeds, while at low 'revs' the slip can be 100% without transmitting any drive.

Preliminary checks of braking efficiency took place at the bottom of Stoneleigh Hill after descents made with the footbrake applied lightly in order to warm the drums, thereby inducing chances of brake 'fade'. The complete absence of that defect was demonstrated clearly by tests which immediately followed the descents when full application of the hydraulically operated footbrake produced a repeated efficiency of 67% at 20mph, with a corresponding figure of 27.3% from the hydraulically assisted handbrake. On each of these occasions the chassis came to rest smoothly and progressively without the slightest deviation from a true forward course, neither was there the faintest suspicion of tyre skid or squeal from the brake drums. Leaving Stoneleigh Hill, favourably impressed by CD650 performance thus far, we took the road to Ryton-in-Dunsmore and regained the main Coventry-London road to make for the Stretton 'straight mile', a test venue used by Daimler and other motor vehicle manufacturers in Coventry. Here the straight level stretch of good road has been carefully measured off and marked by various signs for test purposes, whereby accurate comparisons of performance can be noted and recorded.

The conventional accelerations, therefore, were conducted under most favourable circumstances, all figures being checked from runs over the same stretch of road in opposite directions, thus cancelling out any slight variations produced by differences in road surface or wind velocity.

Starting away in bottom gear and changing quickly into the higher ratios at correct engine and road speeds, the average of two runs up to the speed of 30mph gave the result of 24.8sec. This figure gives convincing proof of the effective combination of a very lively and powerful engine with carefully stepped gear ratios brought into quick action by hydraulically actuated bands on the epicyclic gear drums. Despite the unusually quick manipulation of the gears for test purposes, the engine power was absorbed readily by the transmission with nothing more than an almost imperceptible jerk at the moment of taking up the drive. The second and far more exacting test from 10 to 30mph on direct drive occupied 33.8sec, during which time the engine was called upon for its maximum torque from low crankshaft speeds and a very high degree of flexibility, both of which qualities it displayed in full measure.

For the benefit of those who prefer to assess chassis acceleration from Tapley performance meter readings, the figures I obtained for first, second, third and top speeds expressed in lb/ton were 60, 110, 150 and 200 respectively. Reference to the Tapley conversion tables show that these figures are respectively equivalent to 0.6, 1.10, 1.50 and 2.0 mph/sec.

In view of the high quality of performance obtained from the above-mentioned tests I was particularly anxious to ensure strictly accurate measurement of fuel consumption, lest, perchance, careful tuning of the engine for demonstration purposes had produced spectacular results at the sacrifice of true fuel economy. Here again, however, the meticulous care exercised by the Daimler Test Department was greatly in evidence,

Above: **The driver's cab of a bodied CD650. This particular example was one of a batch supplied to Halifax Corporation in 1951.**

for extremely accurate fuel consumption figures were obtained by use of the Zenith test apparatus, of which I believe only two examples exist in this country at present. By use of a flow-meter containing one-tenth of a gallon supplied direct from the fuel system and a three-way cock, consumption figures can be obtained without disconnecting any pipes or risk of letting air into the fuel system.

An average of several successive trials along Watling Street at a uniform speed of 25mph on direct drive produced the consumption figure of 16.02mpg, which, it will be agreed, is a particularly good result for a chassis with a gross weight of over 12ton equipped with an engine of 10.6litre capacity. Impressive though it be, the result of the straight run does not satisfy the average bus operator for whose benefit further consumption results were obtained from tests on the basis of five stops per mile. A second series conducted on conditions approximating to those of town traffic produced a consistent figure of 7.1mpg.

Both the above-mentioned results may, I think, be taken as somewhat conservative, more especially since later improvements in the induction and exhaust systems give promise of still better fuel consumption. Having now discharged my duties as technical observer and checked my test log to see that no item of performance had been omitted, I changed places with Mr Bob Crouch to experience the long anticipated pleasure of handling the CD650 chassis, thus to record impressions that no mere figures, however carefully derived, can ever convey. Until one has actually driven the new Daimler chassis for several miles it is quite impossible to appreciate the full meaning of 'easy control' as applied to public service vehicles, though hitherto the term has been used freely enough in road test reports.

With 123bhp at his command and the smooth action of the fluid transmission, a driver feels the greatest confidence in handling his charge under all conditions. Even though denied the sound-damping effect of the cab and bodywork, the engine is remarkably quiet, thanks of course to inherently good balance, well controlled combustion characteristics and suspension on 'floating power' principles.

The physical effort required for gear changing can be written off as negligible, for after movement of the small pre-selector gate on the steering column, hydraulic assistance reduces the pedal effort to 50lb as compared with that of 200lb required to compress the bus-bar spring of an unassisted epicyclic gearbox. The gearbox is so designed that in the unlikely event of hydraulic failure, one can resort to normal band operation. The same emergency provision applies to the brakes and assisted steering.

In my opinion the most outstanding feature of the CD650 chassis from the driver's point of view is the assisted steering, developed during the past five years

Above: A view from the rear of the CD650 chassis showing the general layout of the chassis to good effect.

Left: The lower saloon of a Willowbrook-bodied example of a CD650 supplied to Blue Bus Services in 1951.

by Daimler in conjunction with Lockheed technicians. Gone is the Herculean effort required to force a 12ton mass of machinery into full lock for negotiating dense traffic or highway 'roundabouts': with the new arrangement easy movement of the wrist suffices to produce safe and accurate directional control whether the vehicle be travelling fast or moving at a walking pace. Furthermore the oil pressure stored in dual accumulators provides adequate steering assistance when the engine is not running. Hydraulic brake actuation also enables the driver to produce well-graduated retardation for all requirements by very light pedal pressure, thus ensuring safe control at all times.

These qualities, combined with first class chassis suspension, impressed me equally as I drove the chassis along main road stretches at its maximum speed and through dense traffic in Coventry's congested thoroughfares which brought a memorable test of this outstanding Daimler achievement to a satisfactory conclusion.

Update

The Daimler CD650 was launched in 1948, but never proved to be a success and only a handful had been constructed by the time production ceased in 1952. A couple have been preserved.

Test Results at a Glance

Details of Vehicle

Model:	CD650
Maker:	Daimler
Engine:	Daimler direct injection oil engine. Bore, 5in. Stroke, 5.5in. Displacement, 10.618litres. Maximum bhp, 123. Maximum torque, 445lb/ft. Compression ratio, 15 to 1. Governing speed, 350-1,700rpm
Cooling System:	70 flex-joint tube radiator. Fan. Water pump. Thermostat
Fuel System:	35gal tank. Fuel fed to Simms or CAV fuel pump by lift pump mounted on fuel pump
Transmission:	Daimler fluid flywheel and four-speed pre-selector gearbox
Propeller Shafts:	Hardy Spicer needle roller
Rear Axle:	Fully floating underslung worm drive at 8.5in centres; axle ratio, 5.167 to 1
Wheels & Tyres:	11in x 22in tyres all round; twins at rear
Gear Ratios:	Top, direct; third, 1.56 to 1; second, 2.36 to 1; first, 4.15 to 1; reverse, 6.1 to 1
Road Springs:	Semi-elliptic springs of 4in width at front and rear. Front springs are at 50in centres and have 17 leaves with a deflection of 2.9375in under a static load of 5,810lb. Rear springs are at 62in centres and have 12 leaves with a deflection of 4.25in under a static load of 6,550lb
Steering:	Daimler worm and nut mechanism using a three-start worm. Hydraulic power assistance can be provided. Steering wheel 21in diameter
Brake Gear:	Lockheed Accumulator Hydraulic Servo system with hydraulic boost also provided for handbrake, gear engagement pedal and, if desired, steering. Handbrake acts on rear wheels only; footbrake on all wheels. Total braking area, 570sq in (foot) and 364sq in (hand)

General Dimensions:

Overall length:	27ft
Overall width:	8ft
Wheelbase:	16ft 4in
Front wheel centres:	6ft 11.5in
Rear wheel centres:	6ft 0.0625in
Rear overhang:	8ft
Dash to rear axle:	14ft
Height laden:	2ft 1.5in
Ground clearance (exhaust pipe):	10.75in

Suitable for double-deck body, seating 56 passengers under British regulations

Test Results

Date of Test:	3 December 1948
Weather:	Slight rain
Distance Covered:	64 miles
Gross Weight:	12ton 3cwt
Tractive Resistance at 20mph:	35lb/ton
Maximum Road Speed:	43mph
Fuel Consumption at 25mph:	16.02mpg (on main undulating road)
Fuel Consumption with Five Stops per Mile:	7.1mpg (on level road)
Maximum Gradient Climbed:	1 in 10 (Stoneleigh Hill)
Maximum Pull Climbing:	Fourth speed: 80lb/ton Third speed: 180lb/ton Second speed: 240lb/ton First speed: 350lb/ton (not max)
Acceleration:	From 0-30mph, through all gears: 24.8sec From 10-30mph, top gear only: 33.8sec
Braking Efficiency at 20mph:	Footbrake: 67% Handbrake: 27.5%

10 June 1949
The BMMO S9

For many years past the Birmingham & Midland Motor Omnibus Co Ltd has maintained the bold policy of designing and assembling its own public service vehicles with outstandingly successful results, all examples of the range having been characterised by technical features of a highly advanced nature. In developing bus technique in accordance with their own ideas and vast amount of operating experience, the company was among the first to realise the practical possibilities of the underfloor-engined type of chassis of which their latest S9 single-decker with seating accommodation for 40 passengers is a fine achievement in design and construction.

Our thanks are due to Mr D. M. Sinclair, MIMechE, General Manager of the BMMO for placing one of these interesting vehicles at our disposal for road test purposes recently over a typical bus route in the Birmingham area, and although the course was somewhat shorter than those usually chosen on such occasions, the conditions afforded ample opportunities for obtaining all the required technical data on performance. In point of fact, it was quite unnecessary to regard the test as one for reliability and endurance, since models of the actual type have already covered some 13.75 million miles of service on the company's routes.

Before starting away from the company's headquarters at Bearwood Road, Smethwick, the fuel tank was topped up on a level surface which also served for setting the Tapley meters to give correct zero readings, and after checking the gross weight of the bus, we followed one of the routes used by the BMMO Experimental Department for its own tests.

Mounted flexibly by three-point suspension centrally below the frame with the cylinders at the offside, the power unit is so disposed to give an even distribution of weight between the front and rear axles as well as a compact transmission layout. Based upon the design of the BMMO vertical engine, it has a bore of 133mm and 133.3mm stroke having a total swept volume of 8,028cc. At the maximum governing speed of 1,700rpm, 105bhp is produced with a maximum torque of 343lb/ft at 1,200rpm, and the BMEP of 105lb/sq in at between 1,200 and 1,400rpm.

Even at critical idling speeds or when accelerating under load, the engine is remarkably free from vibration or objectionable noise, while its underfloor location allows ample body space for 40 seats without cramping the occupants.

As we glided through dense motor traffic along the Hagley Road, the S9 revealed a lively turn of acceleration and the easy manoeuvrability so essential for operating on stage routes in cities like Birmingham. Although the bus had not been loaded for the test, thus putting the suspension system at a disadvantage, the generously proportioned semi-elliptic springs gave the impression of being able to deal with full passenger loads effectively and to provide comfortable travel under all conditions.

The first of my measured tests of performance took place as soon as we were clear of town traffic, when coasting in neutral at 20mph, the tractive resistance of 35lb/ton was registered by the Tapley meter when the speed had dropped to 10mph, thus affording clear proof of commendably low transmission losses achieved by good design and accurate assembly of chassis mechanism. Satisfied on this important item of test procedure, attention was next directed to the matter of acceleration upon which so much depends in a vehicle of this type in order to maintain strict punctuality on closely scheduled town services. With a lively six-cylinder engine developing a genuine 105bhp at his command, an S9 bus driver

Left: **During World War 2 Midland Red continued to undertake development work on its single-deck chassis with the result that the company introduced its first underfloor-engined model — the S6 — in 1946. A total of 100 of the type, Nos 3000-3099, were built. The 40-seat bodywork was supplied by Metro-Cammell and Brush; capacity was eventually increased to 44 seats.**
S. E. Letts

speed when the meter readings shown as pull in lb/ton were noted for subsequent conversion into acceleration in terms of mph/sec.

With the final reduction in the rear axle of 5.5 to 1, the overall gear ratios are as follows: first speed 25.02 to 1; second 14.9 to 1; third 8.8 to 1; and fourth 5.5 to 1. Corresponding Tapley acceleration figures were recorded in mph/sec as 2.2, 1.6, 0.86 and 0.57 respectively, thus affording further indication of a highly effective grading of the ratios to suit the engine torque characteristics.

can always be sure of a quick and smooth getaway in town traffic, for I found as an average of several tests from a standing start to 30mph using the gears in the normal manner without undue haste, that the required acceleration could be obtained in 23.5sec. Among the factors contributing to this result were the smooth and easy action of the 15.875in diameter single dry plate clutch, nicely stepped gear ratios and effortless control of the selector mechanism.

Another quality rendering the S9 easy to handle in traffic is its really good performance on direct drive for, when running at 10mph on top gear, full acceleration of the engine will raise the speed to 30mph in 15.5sec. Even allowing for the fact that the bus was empty during my test, the figures quoted give a fair indication of the performance to be expected under normal full load conditions.

Further information on the subject of acceleration was derived from Tapley meter tests which, like those already recorded, were conducted on a smooth level concrete road, but in this case were not affected by the time occupied in engaging the gears or in 'going through the gears'. On introducing each of the gears, the engine was 'revved' up to its maximum governed

One thing that impressed me particularly during these tests, was the quick response of the engine to full pressure of the organ type accelerator pedal, the light control of which enables the driver to regulate the road speed to a nicety under all conditions.

Mounted independently in the frame by four-point flexible suspension, the gearbox has constant mesh helical gears with dog clutch engagement except for first and reverse trains. Extra support for both main and lay shafts is provided by parallel roller bearings, while the unit is rendered very accessible for maintenance by being divided horizontally along the centre line of both shafts. Three-bearing support for the gear shafts and accurate grinding of the gear profiles after case-hardening, contribute largely to the silent action of the gearbox both when the bus is running light or under full load.

In addition to being able to move off smartly from a standstill, the S9 bus possesses quite a good turn of speed as proved by the fact that on several occasions, where road and traffic conditions permitted, the maximum speed of 42mph was attained in effortless manner. Governed as it is to 1,700rpm the well balanced engine does not make its presence felt either

Above: **The last stage of the underfloor-engined chassis first developed with the S6 in 1946 came with the S13 in 1950/51.**

Right:
The S9 was followed by the S10. A total of 155 of the type were built with either Brush or Metro-Cammell bodies.

in the cab or saloon while the bus is travelling fast and as the transmission is similarly innocent of vibration, Midland Red passengers can always rely on comfortable journeys when travelling on these popular vehicles.

Long experience in operating buses through the dense traffic of Birmingham's congested streets has taught the BMMO technicians many things about braking efficiency, so effectively demonstrated in the latest example of the successful S single-deck series.

When I suggested to the member of the works Experimental Department who acted as demonstration driver, that he should make an emergency stop, he advised me to sit tight and very timely counsel it was at that. At a given signal he applied the footbrake fully from a speed of 20mph which promptly arrested the motion of the bus and caused the Tapley meter dial to jerk round abruptly and register the efficiency of 75%. The equivalent stopping distance is 17ft and retardation at the rate of approximately 16mph/sec, accomplished with a mechanical perfection which gave the impression that the tyres were geared to the road surface. Of back drum squeal there was never a sign as the bus pulled up as though running on rails.

In like manner the handbrake is an extremely effective implement operated by a business-like lever conveniently placed to take a strong pull which will stop the bus from 20mph in a distance of 26.8ft to give retardation at the rate of 11mph/sec and a 50% efficiency.

For all its effective action, the braking system of BMMO design is of perfectly straightforward layout.

Wide drums of 17in diameter present a total effective braking area of 574sq in, the footbrake being actuated hydraulically with servo assistance from a Lockheed continuous-flow master cylinder servo unit. A three to one boost pressure is provided and the servo control valve is operated from the brake pedal. The handbrake is actuated by the conventional mechanical linkage, but special attention has been paid to make sure that the effort applied by the driver is suitably multiplied.

Figures for maximum pull exerted by the engine through the various gear ratios were recorded during an ascent of Mucklow Hill, near Halesowen, a fairly long climb with a maximum gradient of 1 in 7.2, but that was not steep enough to require the use of the lower gear ratios and consequently it was necessary to apply the handbrake to obtain the required results. The greater part of the hill was climbed on third speed, first engaged rather later than is customary in order to produce the maximum pull figure shown by the meter to be 50lb/ton, as against 46lb/ton noted when changing early into third speed under normal driving conditions. As the climb continued towards the steepest section of the hill, it was necessary to

steady the speed by handbrake application to change down into second speed and at the moment of changing a third-speed pull of 170lb/ton was recorded. The same procedure was followed to obtain the second-speed pull of 280lb/ton from which the first-speed pull was calculated to be in the region of 420lb/ton.

As the recorded results suggest, the S9 engine possesses ample reserves of power to satisfy all conditions of bus service, helped by carefully chosen gear ratios and what may be described as virtually frictionless transmission.

So far, apart from noting technical particulars, my remarks on the general behaviour of the vehicle concern passenger impressions which I must now supplement by comments while at the wheel. There is a grab handle at the left hand side of the driver's cab which I tried to use unsuccessfully and finally got into the seat with a pull on the steering wheel. The cab is comfortable and provides all the necessary amenities for statutory periods of work at the wheel. Gear changing is easy and though quiet, the engine produces enough sound to enable the driver to select his gears by ear, but the position of the clutch pedal in relation to the floorboard encourages the driver to use the pedal as a foot-rest to the detriment of the clutch withdrawal race.

With regard to the suspension, I was pleased to notice that the comfortable travel enjoyed by the passengers is shared equally by the driver, the bus being notably free from the 'pitching' at the forward end to which certain underfloor-engined vehicles I have tested are subject. This I think is all the more commendable as the suspension system does not require assistance from dampers to ensure good riding qualities.

My own use of the brakes was confined to normal retardation for steadying the bus speed, so any violent application was not needed. In ordinary use the brakes require very little pedal pressure and their action is so consistent that one is able to judge braking distances in traffic to within a few inches at any time.

In common with many other vehicles fitted with cam-and-roller type mechanism, the steering gear of the S9 is slightly reversible and rough road surfaces have the effect of producing a certain amount of 'dither' on the steering wheel, but in all other respects directional control of the bus is all that could be desired, both when travelling fast on open roads or while negotiating dense town traffic. On topping the fuel tank at the end of the trial run, the amount required to restore the fuel level to the original mark showed the fuel consumption to be exactly 13.63mpg, which figure included all stops during the journey and a certain amount of wastage occurring while certain of the tests were in progress.

Considering that this test, like all others reported in *Passenger Transport*, was conducted in a manner calculated to reveal every conceivable fault that might occur, the fact that only two minor causes for criticism, ie steering 'dither' and clutch pedal position, could be found, is worthy of special mention.

I understand that the next series of the BMMO S series is to have a newly designed frame to accommodate independent front suspension and something new in the way of rear suspension as well.

Update

BMMO had undertaken development work on single-deck chassis during World War 2, with the result that the S6-type — a mid-underfloor-engined model — first appeared in 1946. This was followed in 1948 by the 8ft-wide version — the S8 — and by the S9 in 1949/50. A total of 100 of each the S8 and S9 models were built; the S9s were numbered 3357-3456. All 100 were fitted with Brush-built 40-seat bodies with the capacity increased later to 44. The S9 had a redesigned front-end, which incorporated electrically-operated folding doors. The S9 was followed by the 155 S10s, 44 S12s — which were 30ft in length — and 99 S13s in 1952. The later single-deck BMMO models differed in that they were of integral construction. No S9 survives in preservation.

Test Results at a Glance

Details of Vehicle

Model:	BMMO S9
Type:	Single-deck, 40 seats
Engine:	BMMO six-cylinder compression ignition engine. Bore, 113mm. Stroke, 133.3mm. Displacement, 8,028cc. Maximum bhp, 105. Maximum torque, 343lb/ft. Maximum BMEP, 105lb/sq in
Cooling System:	Square gilled tube radiator, with a frontal area of 675sq in. Water pump (no fan)
Fuel System:	30gal tank. CAV fuel lift pump
Transmission:	Clutch: BMMO single dry plate 15.875in diameter. Gearbox: four-speed gearbox with constant mesh 4th, 3rd and 2nd speed gears having dog engagement. Transmission shaft: short transmission shaft between engine and gearbox. Propeller shaft with sliding coupling from gearbox to rear axle. Rear axle: fully floating, overdrive worm gear having 7.75in worm centres with four bevel differential. Axle ratio, 5.5 to 1
Tyres:	Rear: 10in x 20in twin Front: 10in x 20in single
Gear Ratios:	Fourth speed: direct Third speed: 1.617 to 1 Second speed: 2.74 to 1 First speed: 4.55 to 1 Reverse: 5.88 to 1
Road Springs:	Front and rear, semi-elliptic of conventional design and shackled at their rear end.
Brake Gear:	BMMO designed, cam operated, with Lockheed hydraulic continuous flow servo assistance. Front brake drum diameter, 17in. Shoe width, 3.5in. Rear brake drum diameter, 17in. Shoe width, 6.25in
Frame:	3% nickel steel channel pressings with channel section cross members. Maximum depth, 8in with 2.25in flanges
General Dimensions:	Overall length including body: 27ft 5in Overall width: 7ft 3.5in Wheelbase:16ft Track — front: 6ft 11. 375in Track — rear: 6ft 1.5in Turning circle: 64ft Chassis weight: 4ton 7cwt 1qtr (complete with fuel oil, water and lubricating oil)

Test Results

Date of Test:	4 May 1949
Distance Covered:	27.35 miles
Weather:	Fair and dry
Gross Weight:	Chassis, body and observers — 6ton 9cwt 2qtr
Maximum Road Speed:	42mph at 1,700rpm
Fuel Consumption:	At 25mph: 13.63mpg on main undulating road, including all stops for tests, etc
Maximum Gradient Climbed:	1 in 7.2 — Mucklow Hill
Maximum Pull Climbing:	Fourth speed: 50lb/ton Third speed: 170lb/ton Second speed: 280lb/ton First speed: 420lb/ton (calculated)
Acceleration:	From 0-30mph, through all gears: 23.5sec From 10-30mph, top gear only: 15.5sec
Tractive Resistance:	At 20mph — 35lb/ton
Braking Efficiency at 20mph:	Footbrake: 78% Handbrake: 50%

Included in the Leyland Comet range of chassis shown publicly for the first time at the company's Kingston-on-Thames factory in December 1947 was a prototype passenger chassis, destined to become as popular among coach and bus operators as are the Comet goods vehicles in the commercial vehicle world.

Now, in the fullness of time, with the passenger chassis in full production, comes an opportunity of reporting on the road performance of an overseas example, placed at my disposal for the purpose, on the occasion of a recent visit to the Leyland Works, Leyland, Lancashire.

With their habitual thoroughness, the Leyland Demonstration Department had the chassis already in test trim when I arrived to conduct the road trials. The chassis, carrying weights totalling 4ton, turned the scale at 7ton 12cwt 1qtr 14lb, as the gross weight including driver and observer. Spare fuel was provided for checking the consumption, and Tapley meters were fixed and set correctly to zero on a level surface.

As the Comet chassis had only covered 94 miles during routine factory tests at the time, the first information required for my data sheet concerned its tractive resistance. This was obtained by allowing the chassis to coast in neutral from 20mph down to 10mph, and produced the satisfactory figure of only 38lb/ton, thus revealing full freedom of the transmission from undue friction likely to impair subsequent performance figures. Incidentally, the low tractive resistance reading provided proof positive of careful assembly of all moving parts as well as high standards of manufacturing accuracy.

Suppressing a temptation to take the popular route to Southport, I chose a less attractive and coach-congested itinerary in order to observe comparative performance figures, the first of which referred to the maximum pull exerted by the engine through the various gears while climbing a suitable test gradient. Accordingly we made for the nearby village of Whittle-le-Woods to see how the Comet would behave on the fairly steep gradient of Shaw Brow, which presents a maximum gradient of 1 in 6. The Comet is an agreeable chassis to handle, ample power being at one's command from the direct injection six-cylinder oil engine developing a useful 75bhp in an efficient and smooth manner. Leyland has succeeded in combining the qualities of inherently good engine balance and well controlled combustion with a very effective flexible link mounting for the unit. Mechanical in action and self-compensating, the arrangement constrains the unit to oscillate on an axis between its centre of gravity and the forward propeller shaft joint.

Shaw Brow was approached at 30mph on fifth speed and by changing gear rather later than usual, the maximum pull on fifth, fourth, third and second gears was shown by the Tapley meter in lb/ton as 50, 80, 180 and 300 respectively. From these figures the first-gear pull was calculated at 450lb/ton, a torque that should enable a fully laden coach to surmount any gradient likely to be encountered on overseas passenger routes.

In addition to the higher performance of the Comet engine, the above mentioned results emphasise the efficient action of the 13in diameter single dry plate clutch and the five-speed all helical toothed gearbox with constant mesh gears for the fifth, fourth and third speeds, the second and first gears being engaged by lateral movement on helical splines. First speed is a super-low emergency ratio of 7.12 to 1; second, 4.21 to 1; third, 2.49 to 1; fourth, 1.55 to 1; and fifth, direct. The selector

Left: **The unbodied Leyland Comet. Its close connection with the commercial motor chassis is all too evident.**

creating an agreeable sense of security.

Satisfied with the general behaviour of the engine and braking efficiency, we next proceeded to a level stretch of main road, clear of the holiday traffic to Blackpool and Southport, where acceleration tests could be completed without hindrance from other vehicles.

The Tapley maximum readings in lb/ton of the various gear ratios, when converted, showed that the acceleration on second, third, fourth and fifth speeds was 3.0, 1.5, 0.75 and 0.40mph per second respectively, figures that indicate the existence of adequate engine torque and flexibility over the full range of crankshaft speeds, as well as suitably stepped gear ratios for passenger vehicle requirements.

From a standing start in second gear, the speed of 30mph was reached through the gears in 30sec, a very useful acceleration factor that renders the Comet quite vivacious in traffic. Under the far more exacting demands for top gear acceleration, the willing engine was well up to my expectations for, when running on direct drive at 10mph, full pressure of the accelerator pedal produced the speed of 30mph in 25sec.

High performance from the Comet engine is derived from technical features that commend themselves to the discriminating passenger vehicle operator. The rigid monobloc cylinder and crankshaft casing is fitted with renewable sliding-fit cylinder liners and provides ample support for the seven-bearing nitrided crankshaft which, carrying a torsional damper, runs in copper-lead strip bearings. Helical toothed timing gears actuate the camshaft and engine auxiliaries, all moving parts being supplied with oil under pressure through a full-flow external filter, no external pipes being used. Leyland precision multi-hole nozzles are fed through an additional large capacity filter, by a CAV fuel pump and diaphragm lift pump; a vacuum governor stabilises idling speed and the air is filtered by an oil-bath cleaner. Producing a maximum torque of 220lb/ft at 2,000rpm, all Comet engines must produce a fuel consumption under full load of 0.385 pints per bhp hour before being passed from their final bench tests.

The first stage of the test was completed by a careful check on fuel consumption for which purpose

mechanism, mounted above the gearbox, has an easy action that greatly simplifies change-speed manipulation with no risk of missing a gear or crashing the gears in a clumsy and expensive manner.

Further ascents of Shaw Brow took the form of fast hill climbs on third speed and a very impressive stop and restart on the 1 in 6 portion, a feat accomplished without the slightest protest from the engine and never a 'judder' in the transmission.

Whether pulling hard under load or under reversed stress, the hypoid bevel axle was equally quiet in action and certainly substantiates claims for silence equal to that of worm drive combined with the robustness of bevel gearing.

Before leaving the test hill an opportunity was taken for checking brake action after the drums had been well warmed by a couple of descents with the footbrake applied lightly. Then, on regaining the level road, while the chassis was travelling on top gear at 20mph, full application of the footbrake brought it smoothly to rest in a measured distance of 20ft with no sign of tyre scrub or veering of the chassis in either direction from a true forward course. A second check by Tapley meter reading gave the percentage figure of 66%, which agrees with the stopping distance obtained previously. Handbrake tests under similar conditions gave constant Tapley readings of 33 to 35%, the stopping distance for the best result being 38ft.

Assisted by Clayton Dewandre vacuum servo mechanism, the Lockheed brakes, with Girling two-leading shoes, give a total effective area of 450sq in. The special cast-iron drums give rise to no squeal under any conditions of brake application, the smooth, progressive action of the footbrake system the main tank was topped up level with the rim of the filler pipe before we proceeded along a main undulating road at a steady 30mph, using the direct drive for the greater part of the run. In the distance covered for the consumption test, four stops and restarts were necessary at traffic lights and at main road junctions and, after a good run for just over 20 miles, the tank was refilled to the previous level when a measured amount of fuel showed the actual consumption to be 24.6mpg, quite a remarkable achievement for a chassis that was not yet fully run-in.

Having now recorded all essential data affecting measured performance, I took the wheel for the remainder of the journey over a distance of some 50 miles, to see for myself how the Comet behaved from the driver's point of view. Despite the fact that the driver's test seat was rather too near the steering wheel for comfort, I found the chassis light and easy to control. Thanks to the convenient arrangement of the three pedals, steering wheel, gear and brake levers, a driver enjoys perfect command of the vehicle which calls for so little physical effort that long distance journeys should be easily accomplished without fatigue. Serving as a convenient foot-rest, the organ-type accelerator pedal is nicely balanced for sensitive control of engine speed and the clutch needs no more than very light pressure to operate. Travel along level and undulating roads is easy work for the direct and indirect gears, the short throw of the gear lever and easy engagement of the dog clutches greatly simplifying the work of the driver. Geometrically precise in its layout, the steering gear is operated by Marles cam and double-roller mechanism, and the lightness of directional control, benefiting to a large extent by the use of hardened steel buttons that take the thrust of the king-pins and stub axles, produces a desirable self-centring action. During my turn at the wheel I was able to observe the perfect action of the steering, both when travelling fast along open roads and through dense traffic encountered in Preston on the way back to Leyland.

Suspension is by short-peened semi-elliptic springs 3in wide, 45in long for the front axle and 60in long for the rear, their action being assisted by Armstrong hydraulic shock dampers. The chassis impressed me as being rather less flexible as regards suspension than I expected to be the case, but this is explained by the fact that the springs for all Comet export models are stiffened to withstand the most arduous conditions of overseas service.

In connection with the suspension and the relation of the front springs to the steering layout, I was pleased to notice a complete absence of that slight instability which so often mars an otherwise perfect suspension system. From his position at the wheel a Comet driver experiences a feeling of steady control by virtue of the fact that the front springs absorb all road surface irregularities, and allowing for the extra strength of the 'export type' springs, the suspension system affords all that is necessary with regard to flexibility.

While the smooth roads of this part of Lancashire provided little of note in the way of gradients, they certainly afforded opportunities for the high cruising speeds in which the Comet appeared to revel. When fully extended the chassis has a most attractive demeanour produced by easy and quick acceleration followed by smooth and quiet motion as the pace builds up to a maximum set by the engine governor.

Towards the closing stages of our test run, we found ourselves travelling in company with a convoy of coaches returning from the seaside and though these were powered by much bigger engines, they were unable to surpass the Comet either for sheer speed or quick acceleration. The proceedings were brought to a successful conclusion by a quiet direct drive run through dense traffic as we neared Leyland to hand the model back to the Works Road Testing Department after a very impressive demonstration of all round performance, fully convinced of its ability to uphold Leyland traditions in any part of the world irrespective of the operating conditions.

Update
The domestic versions of the Comet — based upon a the chassis of a medium-weight lorry — were launched in 1947. These were the diesel-engined version — the CPO1 — and the petrol-engined model — the CPP1. The model tested was an export version of the former. Only limited numbers were produced and the type ceased to be available in the UK market in 1951.

Right: **An example of a Leyland Comet exported is this bus sold to Helsinki, Finland, in 1951. It was one of a pair supplied that were fitted with 33-seat wooden bodies.**

Test Results at a Glance

Details of Vehicle

Model:	Comet ECPO/IR
Maker:	Leyland
Engine:	Leyland six-cylinder, direct injection diesel, type 0.300. Bore, 3.8in. Stroke, 4.5in. Capacity, 306cu in. Maximum bhp, 75 at 2,000rpm. Maximum torque, 220lb/ft at 2,000rpm
Cooling System:	Six-bladed fan and centrifugal pump. Thermostat control. Slack-type radiator. Water capacity, 6gal
Fuel System:	35gal tank. Fuel feed by CAV injection pump with Leyland vacuum governor. Fuel lift by CAV diaphragm-type pump through detachable filter
Transmission:	Single dry plate clutch, 13in diameter. Non-metallic type liners with full adjustment for wear
Gear Ratios:	Top: direct Fourth: 1.55 to 1 Third: 2.49 to 1 Second: 4.21 to 1 First: 7.12 to 1 Reverse: 7.45 to 1
Propeller Shafts:	Two-piece open propeller shafts. Shaft from gearbox to centre bearing: Layrub shaft with flexible centres. Centre bearing to rear axle: Hardy Spicer shaft 1500 series with needle-roller universal joints
Rear axle:	Fully-floating hypoid bevel drive carried in angular contact ball bearings. Axle ratio 5.43 to 1
Wheels and Tyres:	Eight stud fixing. Steel disc wheels. 9in x 20in tyres S & T
Suspension:	Short-peened semi-elliptic 3in wide. Front 45in long; rear 60in long. Assisted by DAS12 hydraulic shock absorbers
Steering:	Marles cam-and-double-roller 24.7 to 1 ratio. Turning circle, 68ft
Brakes:	Girling 2LS wedge operated. 16in diameter drums. Footbrake vacuum servo-assisted operating hydraulically on all wheels. Total braking area, 450sq in. Handbrake area, 264sq in. Pull-on handbrake with mechanical linkage to rear wheels only

General Dimensions:	Overall length: 26ft 10in
	Overall width over tyres: 7ft 9in
	Wheelbase: 17ft 6in
	Front wheel centres (track at ground): 5ft 7.5in
	Rear wheel centres (track mean): 5ft 8.5in
	Back of driver's seat to rear axle: 14ft 0in
	Dash to end of frame: 23ft 7in
	Height of frame, laden (front): 2ft 9.5in
	Height of frame, laden (rear): 2ft 6in
	Ground clearance under front axle: 1ft 1.5in

Test Results

Date of Test:	14 June 1949
Weather:	Fair and dry
Gross Weight:	7ton 12cwt 1qtr 14lb
Distance Covered:	70 miles
Tractive Resistance at 20mph:	38lb/ton
Fuel Consumption:	24.6mpg (at 30mph with four stops over undulating route)
Maximum Gradient Climbed:	1 in 6 (Shaw Brow, Whittle-le-Woods)
Maximum Pull when Climbing:	Fifth speed: 50lb/ton Fourth speed: 80lb/ton Third speed: 180lb/ton Second speed: 300lb/ton First speed: not recorded
Acceleration:	From 0-30mph, through all gears: 30sec From 10-30mph, top gear only: 35sec First speed: not recorded Second speed: 3.0mph per sec Third speed: 1.5mph per sec Fourth speed: 0.75mph per sec Fifth speed: 0.40mph per sec
Braking Efficiency at 20mph:	Footbrake: 66% Handbrake: 35%

10 August 1949
AEC Regent Mark III

Incorporating many improvements, the Regent Mark III chassis reveals high performance and good riding qualities.

As is now widely known, the design of the prototype AEC Regent Mark III was produced just before the war and a fleet of 150 vehicles was manufactured by AEC Ltd and operated successfully by London Transport under the most strenuous conditions throughout the war period. The chassis now being offered to operators incorporates further improvements resulting from experience gained since its introduction, and the model in its present form may justly be described as one of outstanding quality in the field of high quality public service vehicles.

The example referred to in the following test report had only just concluded its routine works road tests and was handed over for an exhaustive series of road trials over the standard southern course used by *Passenger Transport*, without having undergone any special preparations in advance. To that extent it may be regarded as having come straight from the assembly line at the Southall Works after having been loaded with test weights to bring the total weight, including driver, two observers and test equipment, up to 11ton 7.5cwt.

On its arrival at Godstone Green, Surrey, in charge of a works driver accompanied by Mr L. Robinson AMIMechE, who held a watching brief on behalf of AEC throughout the entire proceedings, the chassis was driven to a dead level surface where the Tapley performance and brake meters were set correctly to give 'zero' readings; then in accordance with my usual practice the chassis was examined carefully to make quite sure that everything was in perfect order for an 80-mile test.

When a chassis is handed over for test before having been fully 'run in', there is always the chance of some portion of the mechanism being slightly on the tight side,

thus creating a certain amount of friction liable to impair the performance under the critical test conditions. It is therefore a matter of great importance to apply several tests for tractive resistance to obtain definite information on the subject from Tapley meter readings. Accordingly, the chassis was driven on a level road at a speed of 20mph and then allowed to coast freely in neutral until the speed dropped to 10mph, when the meter reading was checked. My first test for tractive resistance applied in that manner produced the unusually low reading of 20lb per ton, thus indicating a remarkable degree of easy running. Several tests of a similar description gave the same result, which convinced me beyond all doubt that the Regent chassis benefits from a very marked freedom of transmission friction, betokening high grade workmanship and accurate machine work as well as careful attention to all details of design.

For the first few miles the chassis was driven at an easy cruising speed along the winding and undulating road towards Redhill, when from the extra seat fitted up for the observers I was able to pay attention to the behaviour of the model under favourable circumstances. One of the first things that impressed me was the smooth action of the six-cylinder direct injection oil engine which, developing a maximum output of 125bhp at the governing speed of 1,800rpm, rarely needs extending to the full, so that normal cruising speeds can be maintained with the

Right: **Aberdeen Corporation No 49 is pictured in Castle Street on 1 April 1950. This was one of a batch of 10 delivered to the Granite City in 1949 that were fitted with Weymann 56-seat bodies.** *Michael H. Waller*

engine working quite easily. In addition to the inherently good balance and generous bearing areas, the engine benefits greatly from the AEC-Metalastik 'floating power' type of unit mounting in which the common axis of the front and rear rubber supports passes through the centre of gravity of the engine, thus providing true axial movement and eliminating vibration from the chassis. Torque reaction is controlled by a series of serrations formed on the faces of the rear support and any tendency of the engine to move longitudinally during acceleration and retardation is checked by a link between the engine and its rear cross member.

Dense traffic in Redhill gave the driver an opportunity of demonstrating the superlatively easy control provided by ample engine power and flexibility, the action of the fluid flywheel and pre-selective gear selection actuated by compressed air control, to which I shall refer in greater detail later. Owing to road repairs on the hill out of Redhill, the climb out of the town was made over a diversion where the gradient is even more severe, in spite of which the Regent Mark III achieved a faultless climb on third gear after having been balked at the start by some slower vehicles.

After having demonstrated the effective action of the brakes, the driver was instructed to proceed at normal speed along the main Brighton road towards the Crawley bypass, where timed acceleration tests,

Above: **Photographed in 1970, this was one of a batch of AEC Regent IIIs supplied to Douglas Corporation Transport with Northern Counties bodywork.** *David Stuttard*

Above right: **Roe-bodied AEC Regent III No 86 of the combined Grimsby/Cleethorpes fleet is seen on the 'home made' inspection ramp which was installed at the rear of the operator's depot in Victoria Street.** *A. P. Young*

braking trials and other data on general performance can take place under favourable conditions. Before reaching the bypass, however, there were several opportunities for travel at high speed, when the chassis glided along so smoothly as to belie its actual rate of progress which, with the engine turning over in effortless manner, is approximately 45mph.

On entering the Crawley bypass a halt was called to instruct the driver as to requirements of the timed acceleration tests, which, like all others in the measured performance series, were taken in opposite directions on the same stretch of road to give an average for cancelling out any possible variants.

Thanks to the lively acceleration of the big six-cylinder engine and rapid operation of the pre-selective gearbox by compressed air mechanism, the Regent chassis can move away very quickly from a standing start and gather speed in a manner

comparable with that of a trolleybus. The average of several tests from a standing start to 30mph was 17.5sec, thus refuting any suggestion that fluid flywheel action under such conditions is attended by slipping. While these tests were in progress, there were clear indications of careful gear ratio grading to suit the engine torque characteristics and marked ability of the engine in responding to instant demands for full power over its whole speed range.

Even under the far more exacting demands of the top gear rolling acceleration test from 10 to 30mph, the fluid flywheel dealt with full engine torque without revealing any suspicion of slip, the average time for these tests being 20.2sec, during which time engine and transmission alike responded to the heavy demands made upon them in a highly commendable fashion.

Later in the day, during my spell of driving, I found no difficulty whatever in obtaining equally good acceleration figures, thus adding further testimony to the remarkable ease of control which is one of the outstanding features of the Regent transmission system.

Further information as to road speed acceleration was obtained from figures shown on the Tapley meter when, by extending the engine to its maximum governing speed with each of the four forward gears in action, the respective maximum pull on each ratio was recorded. These figures are shown as pull in lb per ton; when converted into acceleration in terms of mph per second, they gave the following results: first speed, 2.2; second, 1.8; third, 1.4; and fourth, 1.1, which, like the other items of measured performance, are highly creditable for a double-deck chassis tested in brand new condition.

The compressed air brakes, acting upon 15.5in diameter drums on all four wheels, now provide a total effective area of 604sq in for the footbrake and 390sq in for the handbrake, as compared with 470 and 313sq in respectively on the earlier models. There are two stages of braking, viz normal and emergency. The first covers approximately three-quarters of the full pedal travel and provides a normal service brake with light pedal pressure. For the last quarter of its travel, the resistance is by contrast heavy, thus discouraging violent braking, except in an emergency.

For test purposes, the driver was instructed to proceed at 20mph and then apply the footbrake fully, as in an emergency, which brought the chassis smoothly to rest without any trace of skidding or drum squeal in a distance of 22ft, for which the corresponding efficiency figure as shown on the Tapley brake meter was 60%. With the generous braking area available, there is no doubt that much higher efficiency could be obtained, but as more violent retardation often becomes dangerous in service I think that AEC designers are very wise in keeping their brake efficiency within reasonable limits.

and the easy action of the AEC worm and nut steering mechanism. A nicely balanced castoring action of the front wheels causes the chassis to straighten out automatically after full lock turns, while the front suspension absorbs all those minor shocks that sometimes find their way up the steering column and cause the steering wheel to dither in an irritating fashion.

Although the full benefit of the AEC suspension stabilising devices is experienced only with double-deckers in service, there were occasions when fairly acute turns were taken deliberately at high speed to bring them into action. Though it was impossible to assess the value of the stabilisers accurately on a bare chassis, I was certainly much impressed by the stability of the suspension system as a whole when subjected to conditions liable to produce some degree of rolling.

For the same speed no undue effort is required on the handbrake lever to bring the chassis easily to rest in 48ft, ie with an efficiency of 27%.

The only other figures required for my test log were those that show maximum pull exerted by the engine through the various gear ratios while the chassis is climbing a suitable hill, but these observations were postponed until we reached Handcross Hill on the return journey. Meanwhile, I took the wheel for the rest of the outward run to Brighton, once again to experience the delight of handling the Regent with its invigorating speed and acceleration, safe in the knowledge that the air braking would satisfy any demands for quick deceleration and have the ability to stop the chassis suddenly in any emergency.

The business of negotiating the traffic roundabouts on the Crawley bypass, normally calling for no little physical effort at the wheel of a chassis loaded to the gross weight of over 11ton, was greatly simplified by quick changes into third speed — pre-selected in advance — a gentle steadying effect of the air brakes

Even for an experienced driver, the ease of handling the Regent in dense town traffic is a thing to be remembered, and as we threaded our way along the congested road leading to the seafront, the chassis conceded nothing to any high-grade automobile as regards flexibility and smooth action.

The homeward journey started from the Pavilion, where the calibrated test tank was filled and coupled direct to the injection pump so that accurate results for the fuel consumption test could be obtained. From that point the run was continued at a steady speed of 30mph on direct drive under nonstop conditions, apart from one compulsory pause at the Patcham traffic lights. A short spell of third gear was needed for the ascent of Bolney Hill and the amount of fuel used checked just before we reached Handcross Hill, where the tests for maximum pull were to take place. Over the undulating main road from Brighton to within half a mile from the foot of

Handcross Hill, the Regent showed an accurately measured fuel consumption of 12.2mpg, which, under the circumstances, may be recorded as very satisfactory.

The fact that high maximum pull readings were observed on each occasion that third speed was engaged gave promise of correspondingly good results from the other ratios during the hill-climbing test about to be commenced. The surmise turned out to be correct, for after a fast approach to Handcross on top gear, the change down into third was delayed rather more than is customary for test purposes which resulted in a top gear pull of no less than 110lb/ton being recorded by the Tapley meter. As the climb continued up the rising gradient, a late change into second gear produced the third gear figure of 180lb/ton. The remainder of the ascent would have been accomplished with ease on second gear, but in order to obtain the maximum pull on that ratio the footbrake was applied lightly until an artificial change into bottom gear was necessitated, showing the second gear pull figure to be 250lb/ton, ensuring an easy climb up the steepest part of the hill where a gradient of 1 in 9 occurs.

From the top of Handcross Hill, the rest of the run back to Redhill was quite uneventful except that it provided further evidence of the high all-round performance of a model accepted by the most discriminating operators, at home and abroad, as presenting the highest qualities a modern passenger chassis can provide.

Update

The first postwar AEC Regent chassis was the shortlived Regent II that was launched in 1945. This model, of which nearly 700 were manufactured before production ceased in 1947, was replaced by the immensely successful Regent III in 1947. Known as the 'Provincial' to differentiate it from

Above: Halifax Corporation 'B' fleet No 383 (BCP677) was an AEC Regent III built in 1949 with a Park Royal 59-seat body. The second vehicle is also an AEC Regent III, but this time a Roe-bodied example from the 'A' fleet. *P. Ogden*

the RT-type delivered to London, the Regent III was AEC's standard double-deck chassis until replaced by the Regent V in 1954 (although Regent III production did not cease finally until 1957). During the 10 years of production, the chassis underwent modifications and the range of engines available also changed. A total of almost 6,000 of the 'Provincial' Regent IIIs were completed and a relatively large number survive into preservation.

Right: Following the abandonment of its tramway network, Ipswich Corporation relied upon trolleybuses to supply all its public transport needs until it acquired its first motorbuses — a batch of six 56-seat Park Royal-bodied AEC Regent IIIs — in 1950. The second of the batch, No 2, is seen in Ipswich when brand new. Sister vehicle No 1 was preserved when withdrawn.

Left: **Fitted with a centre-entrance Roe body, this AEC Regent III of West Riding was photographed at Sandal, near Wakefield, on 10 July 1947, the year that the chassis was introduced to the market.** *S. H. Goodeys*

Test Results at a Glance

Details of Vehicle

Model:	Regent Mark III
Maker:	AEC
Engine:	AEC six-cylinder compression ignition engine. Bore, 120mm. Stroke, 142mm. Displacement, 9.6litres. Maximum bhp, 125. Maximum torque, 430lb/ft
Cooling System:	Centrifugal water pump. Six-bladed fan, belt-driven from crankshaft
Fuel System:	35gal tank. CAV fuel lift pump
Transmission:	Flywheel and gearbox: open circuit fluid flywheel. Four-speed epicyclic pre-selective gearbox. Compressed air actuation. Transmission Shaft: short transmission shaft between engine and gearbox. Propeller shaft with sliding coupling from gearbox to rear axle
Gear Ratios:	Fourth: direct Third: 1.64 to 1 Second: 2.53 to 1 First: 4.51 to 1 Reverse: 6.9 to 1
Brakes:	Foot: compressed air to all four wheels. Westinghouse equipment Hand: mechanical to rear wheels only. Hand lever fitted with trailing double paw Drum diameter: front, 15.5in x 3.625in; rear, 15.5in x 6.5in
Steering:	Worm and nut. 5.5 turns from lock to lock

Suspension:	Reverse camber semi-elliptic springs. Front: 4ft 2in, centres 3.5in wide. Rear: 5ft 2in x 3.5in wide. Torsion bar stabilising gear
General Dimensions:	Overall length of chassis: 26ft 0in Wheelbase: 16ft 4in Overall width: 7ft 5in Track (front): 6ft 4.5in Track (rear): 5ft 9.188in

Test Results

Length of Route:	86 miles
Date of Test:	6 July 1949
Weather:	Dull, dry, northeast wind
Gross Weight:	11ton 7.5cwt
Fuel Consumption:	At 30mph over undulating main road, 12.2mpg
Maximum Gradient Climbed:	1 in 9 on Handcross Hill
Tractive Resistance:	(concrete road) 20lb/ton
Acceleration:	First: 2.2mph/second Second: 1.8mph/second Third: 1.4mph/second Fourth: 1.1mph/second
Acceleration (timed):	0-30mph, through gears: 17.2sec 10-30mph direct drive only: 20.2sec
Maximum Pull (climbing) in lb/ton:	Fourth: 110 Third: 180 Second: 250 First: 420 (calculated)
Braking Efficiency (at 20mph):	Footbrake: 60% Handbrake: 27%

Observant people who cast appreciative eyes on the Morris-Commercial passenger chassis exhibited at Earls Court last year, adjudged the model to be one of great promise for single-deck bus or luxury coach operation. Nor were they far wrong in their opinion for, as the following road test report reveals, it has everything that the most exacting user could desire.

When invited to test a chassis fitted with an entirely new power unit, it is always a good plan to reflect upon its principal mechanical features, and in many ways the new Morris-Commercial engine embodies several notable departures from conventional oil engine practice, mainly because the cylinder water jackets and crankcase are in the form of a single heat-treated aluminium alloy casting, combining light weight with great rigidity. Detachable wet liners of centrifugally cast iron are inserted in the main casting, thus ensuring ample water cooling spaces and enabling worn liners to be replaced by a simple fitting operation.

The engine is of the direct injection type, in which the combustion takes place in toroidal-shaped cavities formed in the piston crowns, a special feature of the design being the shape of these cavities in conjunction with their position in relation to the inlet ports. Injectors of patented design deliver the fuel in conical sprays directed tangentially to the upper edges of the piston cavities, which, at the time of injection, receive the whole of the fuel charges. This action, combined with the air swirl, produces a degree of 'dual turbulence' greatly to the benefit of high performance and fuel economy.

The generous proportions of the crankshaft, supported by seven lead-bronze alloy bearings, suggest great durability and, provided new bearing shells are fitted when needed, no re-machining operations need to be contemplated during major overhauls.

The six cylinders (85mm bore by 125mm stroke) have a total swept area of 4,256cc, and, with a compression ratio of 19 to 1, produce a maximum output of 75bhp at the governing speed of 2,400rpm. The maximum torque produced at 1,750rpm is 167lb/ft.

Many other features of considerable technical interest characterise the new chassis, but as the main object of the present article is to deal with road performance, I will now relate my experiences when testing a standard production model driven almost straight from the assembly line at Adderley Park.

It was a wet windy morning when the proceedings started at Banbury by inspecting the weighbridge ticket which showed the gross weight at 7ton 2cwt, equivalent to the total weight of a complete coach and its full complement of passengers. The prospects of a good drenching before the day was out caused no apprehension as to their effect upon the accuracy of test data obtained from instruments rather than from the recordings of a rain-soaked observer.

Therefore, having fixed the Tapley meters in position and set them to give correct 'zero' readings, we left Banbury and took the road to Leamington in order to observe the action of the two-speed auxiliary gearbox used in conjunction with the normal four-speed change mechanism, supplied as an extra to this model, as well as the behaviour of the chassis in general on the Warwickshire Hills.

On the first part of the journey, conventional tests for tractive resistance showed the chassis to be free from any traces of 'works stiffness' that might have impaired the general performance, by producing a low Tapley meter reading of 36lb/ton on several occasions. Brake tests under 'cool drum' conditions followed and these produced remarkably good results, for, when travelling at 20mph over a stretch of wet tarmac, normal pressure on the brake pedal brought the chassis smoothly to rest in a distance of 16.5ft, ie with an efficiency of no less than 80%, a performance unaccompanied by tyre skid or drum squeal. I was equally impressed by the action of the handbrake, which, unlike some of its kind, produced an efficiency of 40%, and a stopping distance of 33.5ft, also from a speed of 20mph, which is a great improvement upon the figures produced by similar tests of some other passenger vehicles during recent months.

Inherently good balance and an efficient combustion system confer upon the Morris-Commercial Saurer-type engine a highly attractive performance unaccompanied by anything more than a faint suggestion of the all too familiar 'diesel knock', either when idling or accelerating under load. Exerting a powerful pull at low crankshaft speeds, the engine will produce a ready increase of road speed on direct drive under conditions when the need for changing down to third gear might well be anticipated. According to the speedometer, the maximum speed of the chassis as tested was in the region of 50mph, with the engine purring sweetly and giving no indication of undue effort.

Routine acceleration tests took place on a suitable stretch of level road, the figures recorded being the average of several runs in opposite directions with the normal or high axle ratio. Starting on second gear and engaging the higher speeds at correct engine and road speeds, the road speed of 30mph was reached in 20sec. The average figure obtained from rolling acceleration tests on top gear from 10 to 30mph was 35sec, conclusive evidence of adequate engine torque under load at low crankshaft speeds.

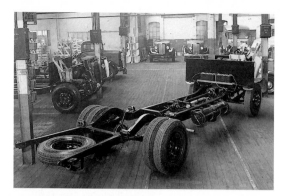

Left: A rear view of the Morris-Commercial chassis. This particular example was fitted with an auxiliary two-speed gearbox.

Below left: Pictured during the *Passenger Transport* test, the Morris-Commercial chassis ascends Stoneleigh Hill in Warwickshire.

With further reference to the two-speed auxiliary gearbox I found the normal high ratio so effective in general performance as almost to tempt me to ignore the lower ratios altogether while travelling over good roads at ordinary cruising speeds. But as one of the advantages to be derived from its full employment is the convenience of having eight forward speeds at one's disposal, I decided to experiment with the two levers to that end.

Admittedly the use of two gear levers involves need for a little extra skill in change-speed technique, but the convenience of having a very close range of gear ratios at one's command soon became unmistakable. In fact, the arrangement may be said to provide a gear ratio to suit almost any gradient and accordingly, if used conscientiously, cannot fail to produce beneficial results both as regards general performance and fuel economy.

By the time we were nearing Stoneleigh Hill, where tests for maximum pull while climbing the 1 in 7 gradient were to be made, I had become quite accustomed to using the two gearboxes with good effect, and it only remained to be seen what would happen when quick changes through the sequence of eight speeds were attempted on a fairly steep hill.

When making the first ascent of the selected test hill, the whole of the eight speeds were brought into engagement, quite unnecessarily of course for climbing a maximum gradient of 1 in 7, but the demonstration served a useful purpose in revealing the versatility of multi-ratio transmission. It will be realised, however, that when any gradient of unusual severity is to be negotiated with a full-laden coach, it would be preferable to change into the low set of ratios provided through the auxiliary gearbox in good time, thus avoiding any need for using the second gear lever at a difficult moment.

Having made a successful trial ascent of the hill, the chassis was turned round for a descent used to warm the brake drums by light application of the pedal in order to apply more exacting brake tests than those recorded above and, in particular, to look out for any signs of incipient brake fade. It speaks well for the general brake design and construction of the brake system as a whole to state that although a very high drum temperature had been induced by artificial means, the figures showing brake efficiency were just as high as those obtained from the cool drum tests.

Next came what is perhaps the most important of all the measured items of performance applied during road test procedure, namely that for determining the maximum pull exerted by the engine through the various gear ratios while the vehicle under observation is climbing a suitable gradient such as that of Stoneleigh Hill. For this purpose the hill was approached with a

Further information about acceleration, unaffected by possible variants such as skill in gear manipulation, was obtained from test results recorded by Tapley meter shown as maximum pull in lb per ton for each gear ratio. These, converted into mph per sec, gave the following figures: second speed, 1.5; third, 0.69; and fourth, 0.29. Quicker acceleration can, of course, be obtained by use of the auxiliary gearbox, but to avoid the risk of confusion, all the readings relating to measured performance were taken while running on the high or normal of the two final reductions.

Whether at high speeds on good surfaces or traversing inferior surfaces, the well-proportioned springs, assisted by direct-acting hydraulic shock absorbers on both axles, afford ample resiliency, thus relieving the chassis from road shocks, ensuring maximum passenger comfort and reducing driver fatigue to a minimum. A further detail that commends itself to a technical critic is the light and accurate steering actuated by cam and roller mechanism with a 20 to 1 ratio, geometrically accurate linkage and the easy castoring action of the front wheels.

At no time during the test run, even when cornering fast or negotiating traffic roundabouts, was it necessary to exert any undue effort on the wheels which, if left alone on straight roads, revealed no indication of 'steering wander'.

flying start on top gear at 25mph, with the engine pulling strongly until the gradient increased to 1 in 37 and at the moment of changing into third speed a maximum pull on top gear of 58lb/ton was recorded by the Tapley meter. The full value of the powerful torque on third gear then became apparent as the chassis proceeded steadily towards the summit, until a change into second gear showed a pull of 80lb/ton as the third gear pull. Second gear was introduced as the steepest part of the hill was approached and with the meter recording a pull of 180lb/ton, it was obvious that a much steeper gradient could be mastered on that ratio without calling for maximum engine power. In fact, to obtain an appropriate idea of the pull developed with bottom gear in action, it was necessary to apply the brake lightly on approaching the 1 in 7 portion to put a heavier load on the engine and then a figure of 350lb/ton was recorded.

The remainder of the journey, still under very adverse weather conditions, brought the total distance covered up to 72 miles which proved that the Morris-Commercial diesel-engined passenger chassis,

equipped with auxiliary gearbox and loaded to represent the weight of a complete vehicle and full complement of passengers, possesses an all-round performance that would certainly more than satisfy the most exacting conditions of service, either at home or overseas.

Above all it has something quite out of the ordinary in the way of fuel consumption as proved by accurately conducted tests with a calibrated tank when the average obtained from several trials over the undulating course at an average speed of 28mph was no less than 20mpg.

Update

The Morris-Commercial described was launched at the 1948 Commercial Motor Show. It was available in two versions: the OP was powered by the Morris six-cylinder 4.25litre diesel engine and the PP by a 3.75litre petrol engine. Largely produced for the export market, relatively few were sold in the UK. After this model Morris concentrated on producing PSVs based on commercial motor chassis.

Test Results at a Glance

Details of Vehicle

Model:	OP/R for 28/32-seat bodywork
Maker:	Morris-Commercial
Engine:	Morris-Commercial six-cylinder compression-ignition engine. Bore, 85mm. Stroke, 125mm. Displacement,4,256cc. Maximum bhp, 75. Maximum torque, 167lb/ft
Cooling System:	Centrifugal water pump in tandem with four-bladed belt-driven fan.
Fuel System:	20gal tank. CAV pump. Saurer injectors
Transmission:	Single plate dry clutch, four-speed gearbox with auxiliary two-speed box
Transmission Shaft:	Two-piece exposed, needle roller joints. Auxiliary gearbox between front and rear portions.
Rear Axle:	Spiral bevel. Four-star differential. Fully-floating shafts. Offset centre case. Ratio 5.375 to 1

Gear Ratios:

	High	Low
Fourth	5.375 to 1	6.66 to 1
Third	8.94 to 1	11.10 to 1
Second	16.52 to 1	20.47 to 1
First	32.47 to 1	39.95 to 1

Suspension:	Long semi-elliptic springs with hydraulic dampers front and rear
Brakes:	Lockheed hydraulic two-leading shoe system on all four wheels. Handbrake operates rear shoes through bi-sector mechanism
Steering:	Cam and roller type. 20 to 1 ratio.

General Dimensions:

	Overall length: 25ft 3in
	Overall width: 7ft 4.5in
	Wheelbase: 14ft 11in
	Track (front): 5ft 10in
	Track (rear) (mean): 5ft 10in

Test Results

Date of Test:	20 October 1949
Weather:	Heavy showers
Route Conditions:	Greasy roads
Gross Weight:	7ton 2cwt
Tractive Resistance at 20mph:	36lb/ton
Maximum Gradient Climbed:	1 in 7 (Stoneleigh Hill)
Maximum Pull While Climbing:	Fourth speed: 58lb/ton
	Third speed: 80lb/ton
	Second speed: 180lb/ton
	First speed: 350lb/ton
Acceleration:	From 0-30mph, through gears: 20sec
	From 10-30mph, top gear only: 35sec
	First speed: not recorded
	Second speed: 1.5mph per sec
	Third speed: 0.69mph per sec
	Fourth speed: 0.29mph per sec
Braking Efficiency at 20mph:	Footbrake: 80%
	Handbrake: 40%
Fuel Consumption:	At 30mph — 20mpg

-Guy Arab Underfloor-Engine Chassis-

Throughout their 18 years of existence, the Arab range of public service vehicles have established themselves as most worthy products of their manufacturers, Guy Motors Ltd of Wolverhampton. Therefore, it was not surprising that we should find the newest Arab underfloor-engined model, when put through its paces over the strenuous *Modern Transport* test route, a most excellent machine and as good as, if not better than, the contemporary conventional Arab models. Most outstanding of its characteristics, in view of the high axle ratio used in the test vehicle, was the flexibility of its road performance, resulting in a high average speed and a low fuel consumption.

We were fortunate in having a fully equipped 40-seat Guy-built body on the chassis provided by the company, as it was a cold day with temperatures of between 35 and 40° Fahrenheit. The vehicle was laden with test weights equivalent to a maximum passenger load, which, including the driver and three other persons, provided a gross weight of 10ton 5cwt 7lb. This load was distributed in the following manner: front, 4ton 13cwt 1qtr 14lb, and rear, 5ton 11cwt 2qtr 21lb.

Below: **An elevation and plan view of the Guy Arab underfloor-engined chassis.**

Horizontal Gardner Engine

The test vehicle was powered by a Gardner 6HLW diesel engine, developing 112bhp at 1,700rpm. This unit is the horizontal version of the well-known Gardner LW series, provides the same power output of 112bhp at 1,700rpm, and is identical in most other respects, thus contributing a high degree of interchangeability between the units. It is mounted amidships below the chassis side-members on twin suspension links, fitted with rubber bushes at the front end and a fully-cushioned single-point rear support. The mounting also incorporates a torque reaction link, and an engine stay. The five-cylinder 5HLW engine is also available as an alternative power unit.

The transmission units comprised a fluid flywheel and a Wilson five-speed epicyclic gearbox slung in an offset position between two of the cross-members. Optional to this form of drive, however, is a standard single-plate friction clutch and four-speed constant mesh gearbox. Air pressure assistance is provided for the operation of the gearbox.

Proceeding from Croydon Airport along Purley Way, we soon got the feel of the machine and found the controls easy to handle, after a short acquaintance. We had started away in first gear, but within a short distance were cruising at 30mph in fourth gear. The steepening ascent required the use of third gear, and with our speed never dropping below 25mph we reached its summit. A free-running

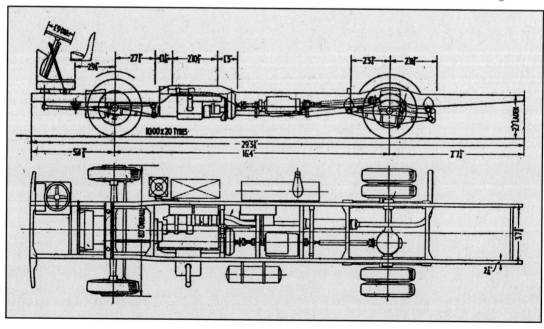

After effecting a controlled speed of 15mph down Titsey Hill, we pulled up on an emergency stop within 79ft from 35mph. This was particularly good in view of the heat developed in the drums and also the existence of a 1 in 25 downgrade at the point where the brakes were tested. As the instruments included an efficient temperature gauge — an essential requirement on an underfloor-engine chassis — we had checked carefully the state of the radiator water during our test so far, and noted that it had not risen above 158° Fahrenheit even whilst hill climbing.

Over that section of the route between Limpsfield and Westerham, which calls for lively action in gear changing and an unusually great amount of steering movement, our earlier impressions of the adroitness of the Arab were more than substantiated. Although having a personal preference for the quadrant type of gear change with pre-selector gearboxes, the position of the conventional ball type of lever left nothing to be desired, especially as the travel from neutral to each gear position is equidistant. It also introduces a degree of standardisation in a model where a crash-type gearbox is an alternative unit. The fatigue of frequent gear changing is much reduced by the power assistance provided by the operating pedal.

Another praiseworthy feature affecting the driver, and a matter in which the coachwork designers had obviously collaborated, was the clear and deep angle of vision provided by the large windscreens and relatively high seat position. Any unevenness of the road was never transmitted to the steering, and the suspension at the front allowed us to enjoy a silky ride over roads that we knew were in poor condition. Later we found that it was a simple matter to write notes at the front of the bus in the position that the conductor might normally assume.

To test the passenger comfort of the bus, we spent the next few minutes as a passenger on different seats. First we sat over the wheel-arch where there was sufficient space between the forward facing seats to allow a reasonable amount of leg room. The suspension of the rear axle could be felt on the uneven surface of the road. This might be all right for stage-carriage use but could be improved for longer distances.

The noise of the engine from a seat almost over it appeared about the same as that usually associated with underfloor-engined vehicles and conversation

descent to Purley revealed the quietness of the transmission components at a speed which was then in the region of 30mph.

For the next few miles through the Caterham Valley — the highest gear used being fourth — we encountered sufficient traffic to make our passage a succession of stops and starts and passing stationary traffic. This gave us an early indication of the excellent manoeuvrability and ease of handling possessed by the Arab. Much of this could be attributed to the delightfully light steering which, in view of the weight on the front axle, performed in a most remarkable fashion. This steering gear is of the Marles double-roller type, with a 28.5 to 1 ratio and a 21in spring steering wheel. It operates through a spring-loaded track rod and drag link, and adjustable steering stops are screwed into the axle ends to prevent shocks being taken in the steering box.

Climbing One in Six Gradient

Avoiding the steep gradient of Succombs Hill (1 in 4.25) which was unsuitable for the high back-axle ratio of the test vehicle, we climbed Bug Hill (maximum gradient of 1 in 6) in first gear, with the engine running on the governor. From this performance it was obvious that there would have been sufficient power to make a successful stop and restart on the steepest part of the hill if it had been attempted. In first gear the Tapley meter recorded a maximum pull of 350lb/ton.

Among the qualities of the Guy Arab was fast cruising. This was demonstrated by its ability to maintain a speed of over 40mph, with the exception of a short section over Worms Heath between Warlingham and the top of Titsey Hill. Although the estimated maximum speed of 55mph in overdrive gear was never attained, it was evident that given a suitable open road such a speed was easily within its capabilities. The higher centre of gravity existing in the underfloor-engine chassis did not affect the stability of the vehicle, and we found that it could be swung about the road at speed quite fearlessly.

Left: The test vehicle is depicted at the top of Westerham Hill after a rapid ascent of the gradient.

Below left: According to the test report, the Arab handled well when dealing with the tortuous roads in the vicinity of Toys Hill.

with the members of the party could be carried on without perceptible raising of the voice. A layer of sound insulation material underneath the floor has done much to control the noise of the diesel engine.

Returning to the driver's seat, we observed that the floor slopes slightly towards the front platform. This has been done to lower the platform height, a height which has already been reduced to a minimum by the irregular shape of the frame side-members. The latter are parallel from the front engine mounting to the tail, being inswept to the front to obtain the minimum turning circle. Over the engine bay the frame is upswept 4.5in and it is arched over the rear axle. This design permits a step height of 1ft 1.75in fully laden and two 10in step risers. We understand that in future Arab underfloor-engine models the frame will be downswept towards the front and the radiator will be redisposed behind the front axle, thereby further reducing the platform height. The minimum ground clearance was 10.9in.

Efficient Cooling System

The half-mile climb of Westerham Hill with its maximum gradient of 1 in 6.5 was completed in 3min 4sec. From a standing start at the Pilgrim's Way, we reached a speed of 12mph in second gear. As soon as the speed dropped to 8mph within 100yd, we

changed to first gear, finishing the climb with the engine running on the governor. On a 1 in 8 section of the hill, the Tapley meter recorded a pull of 300lb/ton in first gear. No rise in temperature was shown by the radiator water or lubricating oil in the sump, both remaining at 62° Fahrenheit and 102° Fahrenheit respectively. One and a half pints of fuel were consumed during this test.

Some fast running was made on the return journey to Croydon when good use was made of the overdrive gear. We found that the latter gear was most satisfactory if it was employed at a speed of over 35mph. There were times, however, that speeds as low as 30mph showed that the Gardner engine was still capable of pulling well. An interesting safety device on the gear lever mechanism is a catch that has to be lifted before reverse gear can be engaged.

An opportunity was taken during the reading of the calibrated fuel tank for the consumption tests, to observe the accessibility of the Gardner 6HLW engine. This unit is easily removed from the chassis by a three-point jacking system which allows it to be quickly lowered and removed from the chassis. A battery of Telalemit lubricators for many of the chassis components is also reached through the left-hand side body valence.

The position of the engine makes attention to the cylinder heads a simple task while the fuel injection equipment can be serviced through a trap in the floorboards.

Two fuel tests were carried out, by making a return journey over a route along the Purley Way. The first of these at an average speed of 25mph was akin to long-distance coach operation and returned a figure of 13.25mpg. This further proved the flexibility of the chassis and the ideal combination of the Gardner power unit and Wilson transmission. The next test was made with four stops a mile and even in this case an economical consumption of 8.1mpg was obtained. From the figures quoted in the table the brakes appeared adequate for bus work where fierce brake applications might prove dangerous.

Update

The Guy Arab UF was launched in 1950. It could be powered by either a Gardner 5HLW or Gardner 6HLW diesel engine. It was originally designed with a 16ft 4in wheelbase, but in 1951 a longer (17ft 6in) version appeared. At the same time the model also became available with four or five-speed constant mesh gearbox; the original version was provided with a five-speed pre-selector gearbox. A lowfloor model, the LUF, was launched in 1952 and production of both the UF and the LUF continued until 1959.

Left: Pictured in the early 1970s, Green Bus, Rugeley, No 25 was originally Huddersfield JOC No 6. It was new in 1953 and was fitted with a Guy 43-seat body. It passed to Green Bus in 1969 and was preserved when withdrawn. *Michael Fowler*

Test Results at a Glance

Details of Vehicle

Model:	Guy Arab underfloor-engined bus
Maker:	Guy Motors Ltd, Fallings Park, Wolverhampton
Capacity:	40 passengers
Engine:	Make, Gardner. Number of cylinders, six. Valves, overhead. Bore, 4.25in. Stroke, 6in. Total volume, 8.4litres. Maximum power, 112bhp at 1,700rpm. RAC rating, 43.5
Transmission:	Fluid flywheel. Type of gears, Wilson epicyclic. Number of gears, four and overdrive top. Form of control, remote. Cardan shaft, open tubular. Final drive, overslung worm. Final ratio (standard), 4.8 to 1; (alternative) 5.6 to 1
Gear Ratios:	First, 4.2 to 1. Second, 2.37 to 1. Third, 1.57 to 1. Fourth, direct. Fifth, 0.755 to 1
Brakes:	Drum diameter (front), 16.5in. Drum diameter (rear), 16.5in. Total brake area, 571sq in. Method of operation, compressed air to all four wheels, the handbrake operating mechanically to rear wheels only
Tyres:	India 10.00 by 20in
Wheelbase:	16ft 4in
Body Length:	29ft 3.625in
Type of Bodywork:	Service bus
Bodymaker:	Guy Motors under licence from Park Royal

Test Results

Description and Length of Route:	*Modern Transport* standard route in Surrey and Kent. About 65 miles
Weather:	Dry and cold
Route Conditions:	Fair
Gross Weight:	10ton 5cwt 7lb
Pay Load:	Equivalent to some 40 passengers
Average Speed on Fuel Test:	(1) 25mph (2) 16mph
Number of Stops:	(1) Nil (2) Approximately 4 per mile
Fuel Consumption:	(1) 13.25mpg (2) 8.1mpg
Passenger mpg:	(1) 530 (2) 324
Maximum Gradient Climbed:	1 in 6.5
Length:	0.5 mile
Turning Circles:	Right lock, 59ft 6in. Left lock, 60ft
Adjustments During Test:	Nil
Acceleration:	From 0-10mph, through gears: 6.5sec
	From 0-20mph, through gears: 14sec
	From 0-30mph, through gears: 31sec
	From 0-35mph, through gears: 46sec
	From 10-20mph, top gear only: 17.5sec
	From 10-30mph, top gear only: 37sec
Braking:	From 20mph to rest, footbrake: 25ft 7in
	From 30mph to rest, footbrake: 50ft
	From 20mph to rest, handbrake: 41% efficiency (Tapley reading)
Estimated Maximum Speed:	55mph

27 September 1952
——— AEC Regal IV ———

An outstanding characteristic of AEC passenger vehicles which makes them particularly suitable for long-distance travel is their quiet and smooth operation. Features of this chassis contributing to this are the direct-injection diesel engine, fluid transmission, pre-selective gearbox and excellent suspension. That the latest model in the range — the Regal Mark IV underfloor-engine chassis — enhances the reputation of its predecessors was demonstrated to us when we tested the coach version of one of these machines recently. It provided one of the most pleasant drives we had experienced with a vehicle in its class.

The chassis supplied was a standard production model which had already completed 233 miles. It was of the now familiar 30ft by 8ft dimensions and equipped with a 4.57 to 1 rear-axle ratio. In view of this high ratio adopted for fast touring work, the excellent performance over the hilly *Modern Transport* route was most commendable. Under such conditions the easy method of gear changing could be fully appreciated by the driver.

Before commencing our test we weighed the vehicle at Croydon with the test load, equipment, driver and two observers. The axle weights were as follows: front 5ton 5cwt 3qtr and rear 5ton 15cwt 3qtr. According to the specification the unladen weight of the Regal Mark IV chassis is 5ton 2cwt 1qtr which, in spite of its extra weight in the form of the gearbox and air pressure equipment, compares favourably with most chassis of this type.

9.6litre Horizontal Engine

In its laden test condition, the chassis had the equivalent weight of about 41 passengers in a fully equipped luxury coach body. However, the all-up weight of the vehicle seemed well within the capabilities of the AEC 9.6litre diesel engine which develops 125bhp at 1,800rpm and we ascended Purley Way at a speed of over 25mph in third gear.

The descent to the traffic lights at the Brighton Road crossing in Purley was used to observe the extent of the tractive resistance. As we gained speed rapidly in neutral gear, the thoroughness of Southall manufacturing processes and testing resulting in the free running of this chassis, were obvious. A light application of the brake pedal at once reduced the speed of the vehicle and assured us of the effectiveness of the Westinghouse air brake in an emergency.

Traffic was fairly heavy on the Eastbourne road and to Caterham frequent gear changes meant travelling at an inconsistent speed. Nevertheless it did prove how

Below: **Elevation and side plan of the AEC Regal IV chassis.**

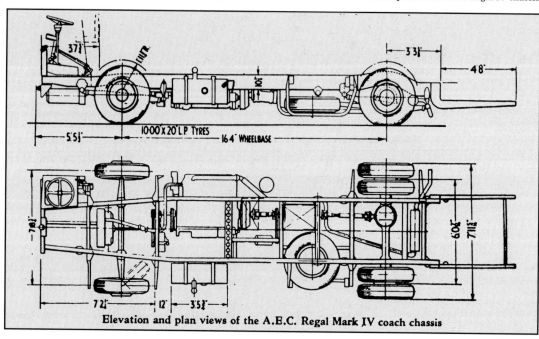

Elevation and plan views of the A.E.C. Regal Mark IV coach chassis

Left: The AEC Regal IV chassis.

and rear also contributes to the excellence of the riding qualities of the chassis. Newton Bennett direct-action shock absorbers are fitted to the front and rear axles.

Owing to the high back-axle ratio Succombs Hill (1 in 4.5) was not attempted and the route followed was by Bug Hill (1 in 6 maximum). Here a nonstop climb was made in first gear and subsequently we stopped and restarted the vehicle on the steepest gradient. A maximum pull of 290lb/ton was recorded on the Tapley meter in this case while during the first test we observed the ability of the chassis to climb the hill without fully depressing the accelerator pedal.

ideal is this form of transmission under adverse road conditions. The rapid and positive gear engagement through the air pressure assistance and a useful third ratio enabled us to accelerate past slower-moving traffic thus maintaining a good average speed. By following the proper sequence of operations and depressing the operating pedal smoothly to its fullest extent, gave us the sweetest drive one could wish for on a heavy vehicle. Jerkiness seemed impossible.

The hairpin turn on to the Caterham bypass from the town was negotiated on a full lock. A 21in diameter steering wheel and the standard AEC worm and nut unit seemed to combine well with the latest steering geometry of the front axle. An extra 2.5cwt over the Regal III has made little difference to the easy handling of the steering, while it seemed to possess the right amount of castor action yet did not oversteer.

Whilst the road from Warlingham to the top of Titsey Hill tends to climb for most of its distance, its straightness and absence of traffic provides an opportunity for fast cruising within the speed range of 35 to 45mph. The ease with which the chassis handled and rode over this section of the route convinced us regarding its suitability for long-distance touring. Even at 51mph — the maximum speed reached at one point — we drove as confidently as we did at much lower speeds.

Absence of Brake Fading

Descent of Titsey Hill at a controlled speed of 15mph without any brake assistance from the engine had a negligible effect on brake efficiency. The air-pressure equipment for operating the brakes and gearbox was of Westinghouse manufacture. Of course, Clayton Dewandre equipment is alternatively available. A two-cylinder compressor is used which provides adequate power for the chassis units and door motors on the

Well-Designed Suspension

Without the body being mounted the stability of the chassis is obviously enhanced. Even so one can feel the steadiness or otherwise of a chassis by swerving, at speed, a chassis from side to side of the road. This we did at about 40mph down the Caterham bypass. As it is intended for high-speed coach travel, stability is of utmost importance in the Regal IV chassis and to overcome excessive rolling a transverse stabiliser is fitted to the rear axle. The use of equal length high-deflection springs at the front

Right: **Dundee Corporation No 18 seen here in Reform Street in 1955, was one of a batch of four Regal IVs, Nos 18-21, that entered service in 1953. They were fitted with Metro-Cammell 44-seat bodies.**
J. Wyndham

A Good Climb

The return journey to Croydon necessitated climbing Westerham Hill. We passed the lower timing point of this hill — the Pilgrim's Way — in third gear at a speed of slightly over 20mph. An early change was then made into second gear followed by first as we approached the 1 in 6.5 gradient of the hill. Our speed at this point was 8-10mph. The time taken to complete the half-mile climb was 2min 51sec. During this test the running temperature of the radiator remained virtually constant at 154° Fahrenheit.

As the figures in the accompanying table show, the acceleration and braking results obtained with the Regal Mark IV were well up to standard. Whilst the brakes were most effective, they were quite effortless in use and progressive in action. An interesting point in the chassis is its low ground height achieved by the offset mounting of the engine. Outriggers can be supplied with the frame for integral body construction.

body. Both the brake and bus-bar valves are incorporated in the reservoir, thus simplifying the pipelines and making the units more accessible for maintenance.

A fuel consumption test was completed on the A25 from Limpsfield Common School to Sevenoaks and return over the same road. Driving at an average speed of 28mph over this rather undulating road — this included two intermediate traffic stops — a consumption figure of 11.8mpg was obtained. As the fuel tank capacity is 35gal the vehicle has an operating range of just over 400 miles.

Despite the difficult nature of the subsequent section of the route through Crockham Hill and Horsey Common to Westerham, the light action of the steering and easy operation of the pre-selective gearbox made its negotiation appear indistinguishable. It is under these conditions, when the indirect gears are being used frequently and the engine is running close to its peak revolutions, that the quietness and smoothness of the unit can well be appreciated. Any engine vibration is effectively isolated from the chassis by the Metalastik resilient mountings. Whilst castor action exists, it is not strong enough to effect over-steering.

Update

Launched in 1949, the underfloor-engined AEC Regal IV was originally designed for a 27ft 6in long and 7ft 6in wide body. This was, however, soon extended to 30ft and 8ft respectively. The type is perhaps best known as the basis of the London Transport fleet of RFs; a total of 700 were supplied to LT. Of these the first 25 had 27ft 6in long bodies whilst the remainder were 30ft in length; despite the availability of 8ft wide bodies, all 700 were 7ft 6in in width. Limited numbers of the Regal IV were sold outside London and production ceased in 1954 with the arrival of the Reliance. A large number of Regal IVs, reflecting the interest in ex-LT vehicles, survive into preservation, although odd provincial examples survive as well.

Left: Dundee acquired a fifth AEC Regal IV in 1954, when No 22 entered service. This, however, was a very different vehicle. Bodied by Alexanders of Stirling, with 39 seats, the bus was 30ft long and 8ft wide. It was fitted with a Johnson Automatic Fare Collection machine for use as a Pay-As-You-Enter vehicle. The vehicle is seen at Dudhope Terrace on 22 April 1954.
Michael H. Waller

Test Results at a Glance

Details of vehicle

Model:	AEC Regal Mark IV
Maker:	AEC Ltd, Southall, Middlesex
Capacity:	41-44 passengers
Engine:	Make, AEC. Number of cylinders, six. Valves, overhead. Number of gears, four. Stroke, 142mm. Total volume, 9.6litre. Maximum power, 125bhp at 1,800rpm. RAC rating, 53.6
Transmission:	Fluid flywheel. Type of gears, pre-selective, epicyclic. Number of gears, four. Form of control, remote on steering column. Cardan shaft, Hardy Spicer open. Final drive, underslung worm. Final ratio, standard, 4.57 to 1; alternative ratios 4.14 to 1 and 5.17 to 1
Gear Ratios:	First, 4.41 to 1; second 2.53 to 1; third 1.64 to 1; fourth, direct; reverse, 6.9 to 1
Brakes:	Drum diameter (front) 15.5in (rear) 15.5in; total brake area, 562sq in. Method of operation, Westinghouse air pressure system
Tyres:	10.00 by 20in low pressure (14-ply front and 12-ply rear)
Wheelbase:	16ft 4in
Overall length:	29ft 5.5in

Test Results

Description and Length of Route:	*Modern Transport* test route in Surrey and Kent; 43 miles
Weather:	Fine and dry
Route Conditions:	Good
Gross Weight:	11ton 1cwt 2qtr
Average Speed on Fuel Test:	28mph
Number of Stops:	Five in 14 miles
Fuel Consumption:	11.8mpg
Gross Ton mpg:	130.6
Maximum Gradient Climbed:	1 in 6
Length:	Half a mile
Turning Circles:	Right, 61ft. Left, 61ft
Adjustments During Test:	Nil
Acceleration:	From 0-20mph, through all gears: 9sec
	From 10-20mph, top gear only: 10.75sec
	From 0-30mph, through all gears: 16.75sec
	From 10-30mph, top gear only: 24sec
Braking:	From 20mph to rest, footbrake: 18ft 3in
	From 30mph to rest, footbrake: 43ft 9in
	From 20mph to rest, handbrake: 28ft 3in
Estimated Maximum Speed:	51mph

Dennis Lancet UF

If near perfect handling qualities and an unusually comfortable and quiet ride for the passengers are criteria, then the Dennis Lancet underfloor-engine medium-weight passenger chassis ranks very high indeed in the range of comparable vehicles currently available. Nor are these its only noteworthy qualities; our recent road test of the latest chassis fitted with Strachan 41-seat dual purpose coachwork, running at a gross weight of over 9.5 tons, revealed a lively performance, excellent brakes and a quite moderate thirst under adverse weather and hard driving conditions.

The Lancet UF, as it is called, is powered by the Dennis flat six-cylinder direct-injection diesel engine of just over 7.5litres capacity, positioned under the floor and attached at three points through Silentbloc mountings. The engine is offset in the chassis so that the crankshaft lines up with the central transmission line and the two cylinder heads and other parts requiring periodical attention are easily accessible from outside through an opening section of the offside body valence. Another commendable Dennis practice is the provision of lugs to accommodate light cast-ring jacks to facilitate engine removal.

Salient Lancet Features

Noteworthy features of the engine include toroidal piston cavities, four valves per cylinder, fully balanced seven-main-bearing crankshaft with Tocco-hardened journals and copper lead bearings.

The straight chassis frame of the Dennis UF is unusual in that it is cut short just beyond the front and rear spring hanger brackets. The front extension is dropped to provide an exceptionally low driving position, and front entrance when required. The rear extension may be straight or dropped and variations of four inches in the lengths (within the overall chassis length of 29ft 3in) of both front and rear extensions can be made to suit the mounting of wide front or rear-entrance or transit-type bodies. Chassis outriggers are a standard fitting.

Weather conditions for our trial with the Lancet UF were not ideal. The outside temperature at the start of the test was about 26° Fahrenheit and did not rise above 30° throughout the day. All but the top few inches of the radiator was blanked off but the engine was still over-cooled and the water temperature generally ranged about 125° Fahrenheit, with sump oil a few degrees less. Even after a mile-long pull, in direct drive, up a gradient on the Caterham bypass, water and oil temperatures rose only by five or six degrees. It appears possible that, in common with many other underfloor types, the Lancet operating in this country will be generally over-cooled. The effect of the unusually low temperatures on the day of our test, which affected engine, gearbox and oil viscosity, is probably reflected in the fuel consumption and acceleration figures obtained, all of which would almost certainly have been rather better under more normal conditions.

The test started with the longish pull from Waddon past Croydon Airport on Purley Way and even at this stage, when still almost cold, the engine gave promise of good slow-speed torque by taking the hill without sign of distress in direct drive. This good 'bottom end' performance is a feature of all Dennis oil engines and further demonstrations of this family trait in the Lancet UF were to follow in plenty. It was particularly apparent in the ability to use overdrive (which provided the very high overall ratio of 3.86 to 1 with a 5.6 to 1 rear axle) comfortably, even in winding country lanes and for short periods in the give and take of town traffic. One further instance which merits mention was the

Left: **The Dennis Lancet UF chassis showing clearly the 16ft 4in wheelbase and the location of the underfloor engine. In the early models the Dennis 06 six-cylinder 7.6 litre engine was fitted; from 1958 the slightly larger 8 litre engine was also an option.**

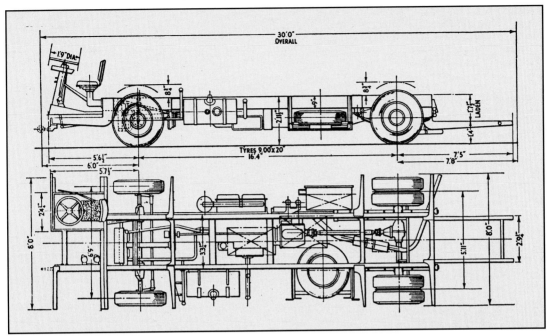

Above: **Side elevation and plan drawings of the Dennis Lancet UF showing principal dimensions.**

ascent of Polhill on the A21 between Sevenoaks and Bromley. From a standing start on the rising approach to Polhill direct drive was engaged at about 25mph just before the steep first bend on the hill proper. Initially road speed fell to about 18mph and we were almost inclined to change into third again, but the engine hung on and thereafter acceleration was maintained throughout the half-mile long 1 in 14 climb and the crest was passed at 35-36mph.

Engaging Overdrive

The first few miles of the test were spent in familiarising ourselves with the controls. We found the low driving position agreeable and the two-way adjustable seat could be put into just the right position for driver comfort and convenience of controls. One minor criticism here is of the accelerator pedal which is uncomfortable for a short-legged driver to hold in the fully opened position without coming forward on the seat. Cab equipment includes an electric speedometer and warning lights in the instrument panel to indicate low oil pressure, low brake pressure, high engine temperature and uncancelled trafficators. Horn, trafficator and headlamp dip controls are carried on a radial arm beneath the steering wheel.

The Dennis two-plate clutch and a hydraulic operating mechanism make a pleasing combination. The clutch is light and, despite the absence of torsional oscillation or torque reaction members in the engine mounting, so smooth in action that it is almost

impossible to jerk the vehicle. Even gross abuse, such as letting in the clutch quickly to start off in too high a gear, results in little more than a gentlemanly shrug and a stalled engine. Overdrive in the Dennis sliding-pinion main gearbox provides a ratio of 0.69 to 1 by means of additional constant mesh gears and dog clutches. The dog clutches are spring loaded to permit pre-selection between direct drive and overdrive, engagement being effected by operation of the clutch pedal, or merely by adjusting engine revolutions after releasing the load on the gears.

The gearbox is generally easy to use for a crash-type box and quick upward changes on upgrades can be made quietly if the clutch pedal is fully depressed to bring the clutch brake into action. Overdrive is mechanically pre-selected by moving the main gear lever from the direct drive position to the right against a spring and then forward — a simple operation, if perhaps unnecessarily heavy. Engagements of both overdrive and direct drive after pre-selection, is quick and positive, requiring full clutch pedal depression and falling engine speed for the quickest response in a change up, and a 'splash' of engine for a change down.

Easy Succombs Ascent

It is not always that a fully loaded passenger vehicle, designed for reasonably high road speeds can be put with confidence on our usual test hill with its gradient of 1 in 4.25. The Lancet, however, made light work of Succombs Hill, first gear being necessary for only the 1 in 5 section over the bridge and the 1 in 4.25 section near the top. A change into second gear beyond the bridge was made smoothly using the straight-through technique and a stop and restart on the steepest section was accomplished smoothly and easily. A test of manoeuvrability was made at the extremely narrow crossroad at the top of Succombs Hill. Good visibility, the easy clutch and light steering added much to the ease with which this delicate manoeuvre was carried out.

Further hill-climbing tests were next carried out on Bug Hill and it was found that a 1 in 6.5 gradient was about the steepest that could be climbed in second gear. Tapley meter readings showed maximum pulls of 330 in second gear, 185 in third, 85 in fourth and 50 in overdrive fifth. Full throttle tests on the section between Upper Warlingham and Worms Heath indicated a top speed of substantially more than 50mph and revealed an excellent stability and controllability at these higher speeds as at the more sedate pace of around 30mph.

No Brake Fade

The brakes on the Lancet UF combine a Lockheed constant-flow hydraulic servo unit and operating mechanism with Dennis drum and shoe equipment. The total lining area of 590sq in provides 62.5sq in for each ton of gross weight, and this generous allowance no doubt contributes to the real excellence of the brake performance. A feature of the servo unit is the incorporation of a spring-loaded accumulator. This provides assistance for three full brake applications after the engine has stopped. A warning lamp in the cab lights up when pressure in the accumulator falls to a dangerously low level.

Our usual brake fade test, consisting of a long coasting run down Titsey Hill with brakes applied all the way, showed a commendable resistance to fade. An emergency brake application while still on the gradient near the foot of the hill pulled the vehicle up sharply and locked both rear wheels on a slightly gritty surface. At this point in our test where handbrakes are often partially, and sometimes completely, ineffectual due to lost motion and the effects of temperature on the linings, the Lancet handbrake was still fully effective. The main brake performance tests confirmed our earlier general impressions and the average distance for several emergency stops on dry, level surfaces from 30mph was 51ft, with a best distance of 46ft 4in.

Tapley meter readings during the footbrake tests ranged from 59 to 64% and the best handbrake-only stop recorded an efficiency of 34%. The average distance of 51ft for the footbrake is equivalent to a retardation of nearly 19ft/sec/sec and is the more remarkable for the fact that the front axle of the vehicle tested was a used one which had already run 40,000 miles without brake relining, and that the rear

Below: **Having skirted the south side of Chevening Park, the Dennis Lancet UF used on the road tests prepares to join the B2211 and head back towards London.**

tyres fitted were well worn so that little tread pattern remained. These results appear to indicate that a reduction in braking efficiency is not inevitable with lining and tyre wear, and that with good design and proper maintenance brakes can still be really effective after high mileages.

Fuel consumption tests were carried out in two parts. First, over our usual out and back section of A25 between Limpsfield and Riverhead, the Lancet covered exactly 15 miles on 7.45 pints of fuel — an average of 16.05mpg — at an average speed of 32mph. This route was rather more free of traffic, and there were fewer hold-ups than usual, although it was not an entirely clear run and the lower gears were necessary on a number of occasions. A second run making four stops a mile to simulate urban stage working gave a return of 10.5mpg and normal fuel consumption in service can be expected to lie somewhere between these two figures depending on the type of service. Overall fuel consumption for a course of 65 miles, which included all the acceleration, brake and hill climbing trials and generally hard driving accorded by a searching road test, worked out at 11.8mpg.

The figures given in the table for acceleration through the gears are averages of four runs, two in each direction, on a stretch of fairly level road. In the runs to 30mph, overdrive was not used but in the 0-40 tests overdrive was engaged at 27-28mph. Tests for top gear acceleration were made in direct drive as it was unreasonable to expect acceleration from 10mph on a 3.86 to 1 gear ratio. Nevertheless, overdrive was used extensively during the test; even in the short runs during the four-stops-a-mile consumption tests, and for short periods in towns between traffic stops, it was possible to use overdrive without having the unpleasant feeling of being over-geared.

Weight Distribution

Opportunities of riding as a passenger in various positions in the vehicle were taken on several

occasions during the test and our impressions gained in the driver's seat of exceptional quietness were confirmed. Very little mechanical noise from any of the running units was apparent and even with the floor trap over the rear axle removed, at 35-40mph the axle is almost inaudible. The engine too is remarkably free of the normal four-stroke 'diesel knock'.

Weight distribution, fully loaded, on the Lancet UF rather overloads the front tyres when standard 9.00 by 20 equipment is fitted. Of the gross weight of just over 9.5 tons, as loaded for our trials, about 4.5 tons was borne by the front axle. Despite this, far from being adversely affected, the steering on this vehicle was the best we have ever experienced, with suspension in the same high class. The confidence bred by these and the other qualities means that high average speeds can be maintained over indifferent or difficult routes without undue strain on the driver or discomfort of the passengers. The Lancet UF is a credit to its producer, highly recommended to operators for its ease of maintenance, simplicity of control, good riding qualities and economy of fuel.

Update

Despite the eulogy that *Modern Transport's* report gave to the type, only 71 Lancet UFs were built between 1953, when it was launched, and 1961 when production ceased.

Right: Having just crossed the A22, the Dennis Lancet UF heads west during one test.

Left: Pictured towards the end of its working life, HJG28 is pictured at Blackheath in August 1967 whilst running on a Brighton-London service. It was withdrawn in 1968; the last of the type were withdrawn in 1971. *R. A. Jenkinson*

Test Results at a Glance

Details of Vehicle

Model:	Lancet UF 41-seat coach
Maker:	Dennis Bros Ltd, Guildford
Engine:	Dennis horizontal six-cylinder direct injection diesel. Bore, 4.134in. Stroke, 5.748in. Capacity, 4.62.87cu in (7.585litre). Maximum power, 110bhp at 2,000rpm; 328lb/ft torque at 1,250rpm
Transmission:	Clutch, Dennis dry two-plate giving 429sq in friction area. Hydraulic operation. Driveshaft, single Hardy Spicer with needle roller bearing universals. Rear axle, Dennis spiral bevel — epicyclic, double reduction. Alternative ratios of 5.6, 6.18 or 8.3 to 1
Gear Ratios:	Gearbox, Dennis five-speed sliding pinion with pre-selective overdrive fifth. Ratios: 4.54 to 1; 2.74 to 1; 1.66 to 1; direct; 0.69 to 1. Reverse: 5.84 to 1
Brakes:	Dennis shoe equipment in conjunction with Lockheed constant flow servo hydraulic operating mechanism. Front, 17in by 3in; rear, 17in by 6.375in. Total lining area, 590sq in
Tyres:	Standard 9.00 by 20 12-ply twin rear. Alternatives, 10.00 by 20 12-ply or Michelin metallic D20 singles all round
Wheelbase:	156ft 4in
Weight:	Chassis, approx 3ton 17cwt. Body (Strachan 41-seat), approx 2ton 15cwt
Price:	Chassis, £2,335 or £2,320 on single Michelin D20s (plus £467 0s 10d Purchase Tax [£467.04])
Maintenance:	Engine, sump 5gal SAE 20. Gearbox, 3.5gal capacity SAE 140. Rear axle, five pints SAE 140. Water capacity, 8gal. Lubrication points grouped where possible

Test Results

Description and Length of Route:	*Modern Transport* Southern route in Kent and Surrey
Conditions:	Very cold and dry
Running Weight:	9ton 10cwt
Pay Load:	Equivalent of driver, 41 passengers and luggage, 2ton 15.75cwt
Fuel Consumption:	(a) Nonstop, 16.05mpg at 32mph. (b) Four stops per mile, 10.5mpg
Gross Ton mpg:	(a) 152.48; (b) 99.75
Pay Load *Ton mpg:*	(a) 43.17; (b) 28.2
Maximum Gradient *Climbed:*	*1 in 4.25*
Turning Circles:	64ft (both locks)
Adjustments *During Test:*	None
Acceleration:	Mean of opposite runs through gears From 0-20mph: 10.3sec From 0-30mph: 23.9sec From 0-40mph: 31.8sec Direct drive 10-20mph: 10.9sec 10-30mph: 19sec
Braking:	Footbrake)average measured distance from 30mph), 51ft. Tapley meter readings between 59 and 64%. Handbrake (from 20mph), Tapley reading from 34%
Estimated Maximum *Speed:*	Over 50mph
Overall Fuel *Consumption:*	For 65 miles of hard driving including all hill-climbing, acceleration and brake tests, 11.8mpg

AEC Reliance

Easy handling at high cruising speeds under very wet conditions and very favourable fuel consumption were features which stood out during our road test of the AEC Reliance single-deck passenger chassis. The vehicle is one of the range of AEC vehicles introduced in October last year designed round the new AEC Series A 410 and 470cu in direct-injection diesel engines.

The Reliance chassis is available with either of the two engine sizes in horizontal underfloor form; it is designed for 30ft by 8ft coachwork with seating for up to 44 passengers with a gross loading of 9.5 tons, and in service bus form has a nominal dry weight of 3ton 8cwt. As a coach chassis with dropped rear frame extension it is 1cwt heavier.

Engine Details

The smaller (6.75litre) engine develops 98bhp at the governed speed of 2,000rpm and a maximum torque output of 285lb/ft at 1,200rpm. For the 7.75litre unit the figures are 112bhp at 2,000rpm and 325lb/ft at 1,100rpm. In general arrangement the two engines are similar. A six-cylinder monobloc cast-iron crankcase-cylinder block houses removable push-fit liners of centrifugally cast iron and carries the crankshaft in seven copper-lead lined thick steel shell main bearings

providing a total bearing surface of over 40sq in. The big-end bearings are of the same type and the small ends of the alloy steel stampings forming the connecting rods are lined with phosphor-bronze bushes.

The aluminium-alloy pistons are each fitted with three compression and two oil-control rings and a fully floating gudgeon pin located by circlips. Cast in the piston crowns are offset straight-sided toroidal cavities in which high-velocity swirl effects are assisted by masked inlet valves. The combustion system is completed by multi-hole injector nozzles fed by a CAV fuel injection pump, combining a mechanical governor and diaphragm fuel lift pump. Depending on the type of brake operation specified, either a Clayton Dewandre exhauster or compressor is driven in tandem with the fuel-injection pump.

Salient Chassis Features

Alternative clutch-gearbox arrangements comprise a 15.375in diameter single dryplate clutch and five-speed synchromesh gearbox or automatic centrifugal clutch and four-speed epicyclic gearbox. Torque is transmitted through a short tubular shaft fitted with

Below: **Elevation and plan of the AEC Reliance chassis as featured in the test report showing the principal dimensions.**

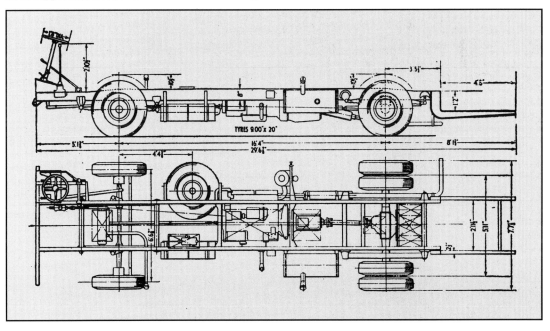

the Hardy Spicer type 1,600 needle-roller bearings, a single reduction spiral bevel axle and fully floating half shafts. Alternative axle ratios available are 4.7, 5.22, 5.87 and 6.28 to 1. Worm-and-nut steering gear is used in conjunction with a 20in diameter wheel and a 32 to 1 steering-gear ratio requiring 5.5 turns from lock to lock. Both front and rear brake drums are 15.5in in diameter, 4.25in wide at the front and 6in at the rear, and operation may be of either triple vacuum servo or air pressure of the diaphragm type.

The chassis provided for the test was the coach version powered by the 112bhp engine and embodying the synchromesh gearbox, triple servo brakes and the high axle ratio of 4.7 to 1. The chassis was loaded with ballast and a visit to the weighbridge showed that the all-up weight with full fuel tank was 9ton 5.25cwt. With the crew of three aboard, this put the weight at just about the recommended gross loading of 9.5ton. A check of the front axle showed this to be 3ton 10.75cwt, or rather over the theoretically desirable one-third of the total weight where twin rear wheels are fitted.

Unladen, the Reliance coach chassis, complete with fuel, oil, water and spare wheel and carrier, weighs 3ton 14cwt, leaving the quite generous allowance of 5ton 17cwt for body and 44 passengers and baggage. A number of finished vehicles of this mark have been produced with licensing weights of less than 6ton, namely the Strachan-bodied 41-seater for Aldershot & District (5ton 17.5cwt), the Charles Roe-bodied 41-seater for Essex County Council (about 5ton 17cwt), and a Burlingham-bodied luxury coach (about 5ton 19cwt).

Test Route

The main observed sections of the trial took place over the standard *Modern Transport* test route on the Surrey and Kent borders, and this was added to by the drive to and from the AEC works at Southall to make the total distance covered just short of 100

miles. The entire test, except for two short periods in the afternoon, was conducted in heavy rain and thunderstorms, and for that reason it was impracticable to carry out our customary measured emergency stop tests.

We took over the controls of the Reliance a mile or two outside the works and, apart from two very short spells, drove it throughout the test. A measure of the general ease of control of the Reliance was the freshness with which we handed it over nearly 100 miles and 8.5 hours later. Our route took us by way of Isleworth, the Great Chertsey Road, the South Circular Road to Wandsworth and thence by Tooting Bec, Streatham High Road and Thornton Heath to the first of our observed sections on Purley Way. Although early in the day, traffic was fairly heavy and this route provided an opportunity of taking the measure of the Reliance in congested urban traffic. We found it a likeable vehicle under these conditions with a lively acceleration, moderately light and very accurate steering with a useful self-centring action, and well-placed controls that came readily to hand and foot. At first the rather small clutch and brake-pedal pads seemed a little out of place on a vehicle of this size, but as we settled down this detail passed unnoticed and we decided finally that AEC is right to use such components of a size (and weight) no greater than is necessary to serve their particular purpose satisfactorily.

On the Open Road

Having checked the accuracy of the speedometer at 30mph against the stop-watch on a measured quarter-mile stretch of Purley Way and measured the turning circle swept by the outer edges of the front wings, opportunity was taken to open the vehicle up. A top speed on the level of 52-53mph was quickly attained when traffic and road conditions permitted and at the higher speeds the steering retained its lightness and accuracy. Despite the appalling weather conditions and roads running in water, the Reliance sat well on the road and open bends were taken fast with complete confidence.

Even on the shinier-looking surfaces on bends without super-elevation, not once was there any feeling of insecurity or sign of a breakaway. The triple-vacuum servo brakes were responsive to quite light pedal pressure for normal retardation and

Right: In 1955 a recent addition to the fleet of Whippet Coaches Ltd, of Hilton, near Huntingdon, was this AEC Reliance fitted with Strachan Everest bodywork. Photographed at King's Cross coach station, the vehicle wore a livery of blue and cream.

Below right: Photographed leaving Burnley on 17 September 1963, this Hebble AEC Reliance, No 195, was new in 1962. It was fitted with an Alexander 43-seat body. *J. A. Ceres*

heavier pressures brought corresponding increases in rate of retardation.

One aspect of control which rather detracted from an otherwise complete pleasure in driving the Reliance was a certain amount of difficulty experienced in getting away smoothly on level roads in second gear — the normal starting gear. This was entirely due to torsional oscillation of the engine and only occurred if the throttle was opened too much for the prevailing conditions before the clutch was engaged and, in all fairness, it must be said that the works driver could not produce a rough start even when he tried. That we were at fault rather than the vehicle is perhaps even better illustrated by the fact that throughout the day we made scores of perfectly smooth starts, including a dozen or more on steep gradients, to only three or four less smooth ones. A possible contributing factor as far as the

vehicle was concerned was the fact that the hydraulically linked clutch pedal was effecting engagement quite near the top of its travel so that there was a tendency to overspeed the engine before engagement started.

Start on 1 in 4.25 Gradient

After general observations of the behaviour of the vehicle under varying conditions of traffic and open-road driving, which had taken us from Southall to Caterham, an ascent of Succombs Hill was made. As well as testing hill-climbing ability, this hill affords an opportunity of assessing the handiness of gear changing under difficult conditions. The four upper gears of the Reliance are all equipped with synchromesh of the inertia-lock type, and the positioning of these on the change mechanism is for a normal four-speed gear. To change into first, which

need be used only for very steep gradients, it is necessary to move the lever across the stop away from the driver and backward.

This may be simple enough on level roads, once the double-clutching technique is mastered, when there is plenty of time to sort things out and no danger of running back, but can be a very difficult manoeuvre, and on some vehicles, due to poor position or length of the gear lever or stickiness of the mechanism, next to impossible; on such vehicles it is often necessary to stop to engage first gear. The AEC had none of these faults. Changing down progressively from fifth to second as the gradient steepened was made simple by the foolproof synchromesh mechanism, and the potentially awkward change into first gear just short of the 1 in 5 section over the railway bridge was accomplished easily using the 'double clutch and splash' method.

Just as important on long hills with a heavily laden

vehicle is the ability to change up quickly on an easing gradient. Changing up to second on the Reliance, once off the steep section of the bridge, proved almost too easy, thanks to the powerful synchromesh, and the engine pulled lustily in this gear to where the first was made without difficulty. The 1 in 4.5 section of Succombs was surmounted with power to spare in the highish 29.37 to 1 overall bottom gear, and stop-start tests on this steepest section both in forward and, during a descent, the slightly higher (27.04 to 1) reverse gears were successfully accomplished. The handbrake held the vehicle easily in both directions.

Blanked Radiator

The forward-mounted radiator was blanked off to about half its depth to simulate the effect of the normal body panelling. In normal driving, both moving more slowly in traffic and at higher speeds on the open road, the ambient temperature remained fairly constant around 60° Fahrenheit, and the water temperature remained fairly constant at around 150°. After a climb of one-mile long Bug Hill, taken mainly with the engine slogging in second and third gears, the temperature had risen to 170°, but fell rapidly to 150 when normal driving was resumed.

The road between Upper Warlingham and Limpsfield provides another of our observed sections on which top-gear performance is studied on the long, but not steep, pull over Worms Heath. In general it

Above: **Seventeen of these Beadle-bodied AEC Reliances were delivered to Maidstone & District in mid-1957. They were designed for one-man operation, being fitted with Deans electrically-operated glider doors and Smith's public address system, as well as a built-in Setright ticket machine.**

can be said that if a vehicle is geared correctly for optimum fuel consumption in normal service, Worms Heath will prove just too steep for it in top gear when fully laden. This proved to be the case with the Reliance and fourth gear was engaged about 100yd before the crest was reached when road speed had fallen to about 12mph. At the end of this long climb, with the engine and fan turning over slowly in the high gears, water temperature had risen to 173°.

No Brake Fade

Our next close observation was for brake fade during the descent of Titsey Hill, when the vehicle was coasted for about 0.75 mile while the speed was held to 17-18mph on the footbrake. No loss of pedal travel was noticeable as the drums heated up and an emergency stop from 27-28mph on the 1 in 7.5 down gradient near the foot of the hill locked the offside rear wheel and, on a very wet road, produced a reading on the Tapley meter of 48%. The handbrake, tried here on the gradient, showed a slight loss of travel in the lever, but was still fully effective.

Right: Another 1957 delivery of AEC Reliances was a batch of 10 received by Hull Corporation. The specially designed front entrance/centre exit 40-seat bodywork was manufactured by MVC at its Weymann works in Addlestone.

As the roads were wet throughout the day our normal measured emergency stops using the electrically operated chalk-firing magazine were impracticable. For this reason, whenever the roads showed a little less wet or signs of a good matt surface under the wet and traffic conditions were suitable, emergency stops were made and Tapley meter readings recorded. The average of readings for footbrake stops from 30mph was about 60% and for handbrake-only stops from 20mph about 30%, showing promise of really powerful braking under dry conditions.

Sparkling Acceleration

What is likely to prove an endearing quality to the many future drivers of the Reliance is its really smart acceleration for a vehicle with a high axle ratio. The figures shown in the table of 10.6 and 18.4sec through the gears from rest to 20 and 30mph respectively were obtained on a nearly level stretch of the Great Chertsey Road and are the averages of four runs, two in each direction, for each result. The top gear acceleration was smooth and fuss-free from 10mph and the figures given are averages of two runs in opposite directions.

The main fuel consumption test under nonstop give-and-take conditions was carried out over our usual 7.5-mile stretch of the A25 between Limpsfield Common and Rivershead, covered in both directions. Although traffic was not quite as heavy as usual there were a number of checks in the villages on the route, and the Reliance covered the 15 miles at an average speed of 28.1mph for a fuel consumption of 15.7mpg. Both figures would have been even more favourable if it had not been necessary to stop to retrieve one of the crew's hat, which had been whipped off by a gust of wind.

Stage Service Operation

That the Reliance will show equally favourable fuel consumption on stage carriage operation is indicated by the result of our four-stops-a-mile test, which was undertaken on a section of the A240 taking in Epsom and Ewell.

Stops were made approximately every quarter of a mile, and these were found to correspond very closely with the actual stops on London Transport country services route No 406. Indeed, for a distance of about two miles, we were actually running in convoy with a London Transport double-decker, stopping when it did — though not in a position as to be a nuisance at the stops — before finally overtaking it by reason of our superior acceleration. Fuel consumption, measured by flowmeter, during this test worked out at a very advantageous 13.2mpg.

Perhaps most remarkable of all was the overall fuel consumption. For 96 miles which, although it was a little less severe because of weather conditions than it might otherwise have been, consisted of mainly hard driving, numerous stops, acceleration and hill-climbing tests and about 20 miles of heavy urban traffic, the very surprising figure of 15.7mpg was returned.

Below: The following year, Hull's neighbour across the Humber, Grimsby/Cleethorpes, also acquired two-door AEC Reliances. This was a batch of six vehicles fitted with Roe bodies. In addition to 41 seated passengers, the buses were also designed to take 17 standing passengers.

Update

The AEC Reliance was launched in 1953 as a lightweight underfloor-engined single-deck chassis. Over the years it underwent a number of modifications in terms of wheelbase, engine unit and gearbox. Production of the type continued up until the final demise of AEC in 1979, by which stage it had been transformed into a heavyweight coach chassis.

Left: Douglas Corporation No 33 is pictured in 1972 in its home town. This was one of two — Nos 32 and 33 — supplied in 1958 fitted with Mulliner 42-seat bodies.
David Stuttard

Test Results at a Glance

Details of Vehicle

Model:	Reliance coach chassis
Maker:	AEC Ltd, Southall, Middlesex
Engine:	AEC AH470 direct-injection diesel. Bore, 4.4094in. Stroke, 5.1181in. Capacity, 469cu in (7.685litre). Maximum power, 112bhp at 2,000rpm; 320lb/ft torque at 1,100rpm
Transmission:	Clutch: single dryplate, 15.375in diameter and 237sq in friction area. Driveshaft: short open tubular shaft with Hardy Spicer type 1,600 needle roller universals. Rear axle: single-reduction spiral bevel with fully floating shafts, ratio 4.7 to 1. Alternatives 5.22 to 1, 5.87 to 1 and 6.28 to 1 can be supplied
Gear Ratios:	Five-speed gearbox with inertia lock synchromesh on four highest gears. Ratios: 6.25 to 1; 4.4 to 1; 2.65 to 1; direct. Reverse, 6.01 to 1
Brakes:	Clayton Dewandre triple servo with Girling cam-operated shoe equipment. Drums, (front) 15.5in diameter by 4.5in wide and (rear) 15.5in diameter by 6in wide. Total lining area 618sq in; rear only, 362sq in. Handbrake mechanical to rear wheels only
Tyres:	9.00 by 20 10-ply, twin rear
Wheelbase:	16ft 4in
Weight:	Dry, 3ton 9cwt. With fuel, oil, water, spare wheel and carrier, 3ton 14cwt

Test Results

Description and Length of Route:	Mainly *Modern Transport* Southern route in Kent and Surrey
Conditions:	Continuous heavy rain throughout the day
Running Weight:	9ton 5.25cwt plus crew of three
Pay Load:	3ton 13cwt allows 2ton 8cwt for body
Fuel Consumption:	(a) Nonstop 15.7mpg at 28.1mph average speed. (b) Four stops per mile 13.2mpg
Gross Ton mpg:	(a) 149.15; (b) 125.4
Pay Load Ton mpg:	(a) 57.3; (b) 48.2
Maximum Gradient Climbed:	1 in 4.25
Turning Circles:	69ft on both locks
Adjustments During Test:	None
Acceleration:	Through gears mean of opposite runs: From 0-20mph: 10.6sec From 0-30mph: 18.4sec Top gear only 10-20mph: 11.4sec 10-30mph: 25.4sec
Braking:	Weather conditions unsuitable for making measured stops. Tapley meter readings ranged around 60% with footbrake and 25-30% with handbrake only
Estimated Maximum Speed:	52-53mph
Overall Fuel Consumption:	For 96 miles of mainly hard driving, including 25 miles of London suburbs, 15.7mpg

Bedford/Duple Service Bus

The combined efforts of Vauxhall Motors and Duple Motor Bodies have always produced some first class buses and coaches at economical prices. With their attractive lines, long life and backed by excellent service facilities, large and small operators alike have found these vehicles invaluable for many kinds of duty. Now the two companies are marketing a diesel engined 40-seater service bus for £3,000 complete, which must surely be one of the best investments in motor vehicles today. This should appeal particularly to the rural operator with fluctuating traffic where it would serve a useful purpose for school and works contracts, market day services or even private hire.

Perkins Diesel Engine

Based on the Bedford SB-type passenger chassis, it is powered by a Perkins R6 diesel engine developing 108bhp at 2,700rpm. The drive is transmitted through a single dry plate clutch of 12in diameter to a four-speed gearbox which has synchromesh on the upper three ratios. There is a hypoid final drive and fully floating axle shaft, the back axle ratio being 5.833 to 1; an Eaton two-speed axle is available if required. All other chassis are the same as those employed in the Vega coach model which was tested and described in our issue of 10 February 1954.

The overall length of the bus is 30ft and it has a width of 8ft, which appears to provide ample room for 40 passengers, which can be accommodated on either service bus or semi-luxury seats. If a wider door is used the seating capacity is reduced to 39 passengers.

The all-metal body is of a lightweight pattern specially designed by Duple for the exacting conditions of stage carriage work. It has a forward

Below: **Very wet conditions existed during the fuel consumption test over a distance of 44 miles. The bus is seen here passing through Biggleswade Market Place.**

entrance with a folding manually worked door which leads on to a spacious platform behind the driver's cab. The emergency exit consists of a hinged door directly opposite the entrance. The seats all face forward, those from the rear wheel-arches to the back being on a raised platform, with a full width seat at the rear. For lightness the seat frames are of the Accles and Pollock Dapta type. There are half-sliding windows of the Widney Cresta type fitted to all the full-sized windows, while the full length cantilever parcel racks are fitted as an optional extra. Lights and extractor ventilators are fitted in the roof.

Poor Weather Conditions

When I took over the bus for testing at the Vauxhall Works, Luton, the weather was as unpleasant as it could be and remained so for the remainder of the day. The temperature in the open was about 45° Fahrenheit and in the hope that things might improve in this matter, I decided to proceed on a long fuel consumption test which might be equivalent to the type of service performed by a rural operator. It would also give me some general impressions of the vehicle's behaviour.

Before leaving the works I had the laden bus weighed and obtained the following figures: total weight, 7ton 11cwt; front axle load, 2ton 17cwt 3qtr; and rear axle load, 4ton 14cwt 3qtr. This demonstrator, which only had seats for 39 passengers, had already recorded on the speedometer a mileage of 4,426.

Except for the fact that this service bus was not equipped with a two-speed rear axle, it had similar features to the Bedford Vega coach which I had tested earlier and had a gross weight of only 4cwt 2qtr less, so I anticipated a rather similar performance for each machine. The 24V starting equipment made no fuss

of bringing the Perkins engine into life and I was told by the demonstration driver that it had started just as easily without the aid of the Kigass pump when quite cold.

Hill-Climbing Capabilities

I directed the bus on to the Luton-Hitchin road, which for a main thoroughfare is narrow and winding. There is a gradient of 1 in 8.5 up to Stopsley, and I had to go through the gears from top to second, finally ascending at a speed of 12mph. Such an operation presented no difficulty for, not only was I already well acquainted with this particular type of gearbox, but the synchromesh on each of these ratios seems almost crash-proof. The cones seem capable of synchronising under the quickest movement of the gear lever.

Proceeding towards Hitchin, I was well satisfied with the driving position and the good view of the road ahead and to the nearside. I found that width and turns could be comfortably judged despite the fact that the driver's seat is positioned farther back than one is accustomed to on the latest underfloor and rear-engined chassis.

Fuel Consumption

Passing through Hitchin and Henlow, we eventually arrived at Biggleswade, whence we returned over the same route to Luton, covering an overall distance of 44 miles in 1hr 44min. A fuel consumption figure of 13.4mpg was obtained at an average speed of 25.4mph. This may seem a rather high consumption in view of the fact that only three stops occurred during the trip but the weather conditions were extremely bad and the engine was running well below its normal temperature. A top tank thermometer reading gave 94° Fahrenheit — a figure which should obviously be in the region of 120° Fahrenheit.

During the last section of the run Offley Hill, with a gradient of 1 in 8, was climbed effortlessly in second gear at 10mph. Frequently when in top gear I had to change into a lower grade on gradients that I felt should not have required it, giving the impression that the bus was slightly underpowered. Such a demonstration of efficiency, however, on the last hill — the steepest climbed during the test — was sufficient assurance that at least the overall ratios of the lower gears were adequate for all needs. The gearbox and back axle units, of course, are identical to those used for the petrol-engined version of the bus; the latter incidentally costs £2,575.

The rain was still intense when I carried out the braking tests along Park Street, Luton. The road is as level as one can find in this area and readings were

Above: **The interior of the bus is free from stanchions, while the full-length cantilever luggage racks were, according to the test report, useful for rural services.**

taken on a Tapley meter in both directions. With the vacuum servo hydraulic equipment used on these Bedford buses, brake retardation was safe and smooth. From a speed of 30mph an efficiency of 63.5% was recorded — an average figure for the two directions — while from 20mph I obtained a figure of 65%. Both figures are equivalent to a stopping distance of approximately 21ft. The handbrake I had tested previously on a gradient of 1 in 8.5, where little effort was required in bringing the bus to rest from a rolling speed of 12mph and holding it there. With dry road conditions these results most certainly could have been improved upon, bringing them nearer the figure of about 70% obtained with the Vega coach on a dry road.

Then followed the acceleration tests over the same stretch of road. Using all four gears a speed of 20mph from rest was reached in 18.5sec and 30mph in 35sec. This was considerably better than the results obtained with the coach. In top gear it took only 17sec to

accelerate from 10mph to 20mph and 34sec to reach a speed of 30mph. These figures rather dispelled my earlier views on the insufficiency of power in top gear.

To assess the value of the bus on urban stage carriage service I finally drove it over one of the Luton Corporation Transport routes. This was route No 4 from the Skimpot, on the Dunstable road, to Stopsley, considered the severest in the district, as there is a 1 in 8.5 gradient among the many hills that are negotiated. Starting from the Skimpot end of the route, 15sec stops were made at many of the regular points and for the round journey we averaged four stops per mile and a speed of 15.3mph. During this test the fuel consumption worked out at 11.2mpg.

This was only a short run, but sufficient to indicate that the controls are light enough to prevent fatigue under a long spell of bus driving. The clutch, gearbox and steering are a pleasure to handle, while the suspension is well up to Bedford standard. Only the noise of the diesel engine was irritating to me, and I felt that more sound insulation in the engine cowl would be an improvement. The noise is certainly obvious in the front passenger seats, but hardly discernible from the third row of seats. This may be acceptable to short distance passengers but can hardly be pleasant on longer journeys.

Update

The Bedford-Duple Service Bus was a stage carriage verion of the Bedford SB (see also Super Vega on pp97-100). It was fitted with a Duple all-metal body. Duple had acquired Nudd Bros & Lockyer Ltd of Kegworth during 1955 and had retitled it Duple Metal Bodies (Midland) Ltd and this concern specialised on the metal-framed bodies.

Left: **The Bedford/Duple service bus is seen on test in Luton beside a Luton Corporation double-decker at the Skimpot terminus.**

Brief Details of the Bedford SB Diesel Engine Chassis

Diesel Engine:	Perkins R6. Number of cylinders, six. Bore, 4in. Stroke, 4.5in. Capacity, 339.3cu in. Maximum bhp, 108 at 2,700rpm. Compression ratio, 1.75 to 1	*Steering:*	Semi-irreversible worm and sector, ratio 26 to 1. Turning circle diameter, 64ft 6in
Clutch:	Single dry plate. 12in nominal diameter	*Electrical Equipment:*	24V starting and lighting. Four 6V batteries, 114amp/hr and 20hr rate
Gearbox:	Four forward speeds. Synchromesh on top, third and second. Ratios: first, 7.06 to 1; second, 3.332 to 1; third, 1.711 to 1; fourth, direct; reverse, 7.06 to 1	*Wheels and Tyres:*	Pressed steel wheels, B6.00 by 20, 5.1in offset. Tyres 8.25-20, 12 ply. Optional tyres, 9.00-20, 10 ply on B.65 by 20, 6.5in offset wheels
		Fuel Tank:	Capacity 26gal
Rear Axle:	Fully floating, hypoid drive. Ratios: 6/35 (5.833 to 1) or 5/34 (6.8 to 1). Eaton two-speed axle optional; ratios, 4.89 to 1 and 6.8 to 1.	*Frame:*	Deep channel section side-members, tapered towards front and rear, riveted to cross-members by cold squeeze process. Horizontal section of front cross-member bolted and detachable for easy removal of power unit assembly. Six cross-members
Brakes:	Hydraulic on all four wheels, with pressure-reaction vacuum servo assistance. Vacuum exhauster fitted with diesel option. Total lining area 498.5sq in. Pull up type handbrake operates rear brakes mechanically	*Springs:*	Semi-elliptic springs front and rear, 45in long and 2.25in wide

13 July 1955
The Rowe Hillmaster

Such are the problems that characterise the operation of public service vehicles in the West Country that one operator in Cornwall, M. G. Rowe Motors (Doublebois) Ltd, of Dobwalls, near Liskeard, decided about two years ago to embark upon the manufacturing side of the industry. This resulted in the production of the Rowe Hillmaster, a modern underfloor-engined passenger chassis which has many interesting features and a remarkable economy and performance. After 12 months in the service of this builder-operator, covering many thousands of miles on excursions, tours and long distance private hire runs, the chassis fully came up to the expectations of its progenitor, Mr M. G. Rowe, who, with the present full scale production of the model, is making it readily available to the transport industry. I was fortunate enough recently to make a road test on the prototype coach during one of its regular trips to London.

The present model is the result of several years of development work based on a vertical engine version of the chassis. On a wheelbase of 17ft, the Hillmaster has been designed to have an overall length of 28ft. The prototype model which I tested was equipped with a Whitson 37-seat composite body which had the overall dimensions of 28ft long and 7ft 6in wide. The narrowness of the Cornish roads has rather influenced the design of the chassis and resulted in these smaller than usual dimensions; later models will almost certainly be available with the full 8ft wide dimensions where they are required for districts that are not so restricted.

The chassis frame is near to conventional with deep channel section side-members and six robust cross-members bolted to the frame. This has a flat top except at the rear end, where the extension beyond the wheel-arch is dropped to accommodate a large luggage boot. The frame is, however, exceptional for the way that the engine is mounted within the frame members by sweeping them out around the unit. Whilst this has tended to throw the transmission line off centre it has enabled the engine to be well placed and make it accessible from trapdoors in the centre gangway of the body; it has also helped to reduce the chassis frame height from the ground, which in the case of the Hillmaster is only 2ft 10.5in when unladen.

One of the most interesting features of this vehicle is the power unit, which is a Meadows 4 DC330 model adapted for horizontal mounting. Mr Rowe was the first person to employ this engine in such a manner and was responsible for the modifications necessary to make it suitable for his chassis. These include such items as a modified sump and inlet manifold. So successful has this been that Henry Meadows Ltd, the manufacturers of the engine, are now making a 4 HDC unit which is the production model based on Mr Rowe's modifications. The transmission is taken through a 14in diameter Borg & Beck clutch to another Meadows unit, in this case a five-speed gearbox with constant mesh on four ratios, and an overdrive for the top gear. A Hardy Spicer propeller shaft then transmits the drive to a Moss spiral bevel rear axle which has a ratio of 6.166 to 1.

It was a fair day when I took over the Hillmaster for test in company with Mr Rowe. The coach had done approximately 6,000 miles and was loaded with sandbags weighing 2ton. This gave us a gross weight of 7ton 11cwt, the unladen weight of the chassis being 5ton 8cwt, while 3cwt was allowed for the driver and observer. When weighed, the coach showed that the load was distributed as follows: front axle, 2ton 8cwt

Below: **The Rowe Hillmaster chassis was announced in 1954. Advertising at the time claimed the chassis to be 'Lightest • Fastest • Most Economical underfloor-engined chassis of its class'.**

Above: **The power unit in the prototype Rowe Hillmaster was provided by a Meadows horizontal four-cylinder engine.**

High Speed Cruising

As I proceeded along the Purley Way full advantage was taken of the overdrive gear and we were travelling in the region of 50mph until the gradient alongside the Croydon Airport was reached. Here speed was reduced and it was necessary to change down into fourth gear, the long and tedious gradient being ascended at a maximum speed of 23mph. The liveliness of the brakes was apparent as we descended towards the traffic lights at the Purley crossroads; they seemed to respond to the lightest touch of the pedal. The next test for the Hillmaster was the climb of Succombs Hill with its maximum gradient of 1 in 4.5. Starting in second gear the ratio was retained until the 1 in 5 section had been cleared, when third gear was engaged. But as the maximum gradient was approached it was necessary to change down first to the second gear and finally to the bottom gear; ascending this section the coach had a speed of approximately 8mph on half throttle. The descent revealed that the handbrake of the Hillmaster was capable of holding it on gradients of the utmost severity. So many hills in Cornwall might demand a stop and restart under difficult circumstances that I decided to make a test of this strenuous nature on the 1 in 4.5 section. A smooth co-ordination of the controls and the power of the engine enabled a smooth and rapid getaway to be made. Throughout these hill climbs the radiator temperature had risen from 135° Fahrenheit to only 138°, and I found that the temperature remained at the lower figure during the whole test. The ambient temperature for the day was in the region of 50° Fahrenheit.

Fuel Consumption

The good fuel consumption for which the vehicle is renowned was confirmed during the test which we made along the Eastbourne road from the London end of the Caterham bypass to Felbridge, just north of East Grinstead. Over a return journey covering 23 miles at an average speed of 25mph with no stops, the Hillmaster returned a fuel consumption of 29.25mpg. With a tank capacity of 18gal, this would give the vehicle a range of well over 500 miles. With such a result as this the Hillmaster would obviously give a fuel consumption on the right side of 20mpg when used on an average long-distance journey in this country.

Acceleration and brake tests were made on a level stretch of road near Mitcham Common. From rest I accelerated through all the gears to 20mph in 10sec, while 30mph took 27sec. For the acceleration in one gear only, the fourth gear ratio was used and from 10 to 20mph the time taken was 10sec, while 30mph was reached in 21sec. Good brake figures were not really obtainable because the road conditions were wet and inclined to be treacherous, but from 30mph the footbrake recorded a reading of 48% on the Tapley meter, while from 20mph the figure was 50%, which, for the conditions that existed and the fully laden

3qtr; rear axle, 5ton 2cwt 2qtr. As the vehicle had been designed for hilly country it was decided to take it to an area where I knew that severe gradients existed. So I directed the coach towards south London and the area around the Caterham Valley. My immediate impression was one of comfort, smooth running and quietness. Some rather uneven roads in some of the London suburban areas caused no discomfort, and the engine was commendably quiet for a four-cylinder diesel unit. Rainy conditions were encountered as we passed through the Streatham and Brixton area and traffic made me drive slowly. This part of the route did not give me the opportunity to use overdrive gear at all and I was using fourth and third ratios for most of the time. It was not until we turned on to Mitcham Common and the Purley Way that any use could be made of the higher gear.

Although the arrangement and layout of the gear change was not all that could be desired, one soon became accustomed to its use and movement enabling quick and quiet gear changes to be made. The steering on the other hand was excellent, both on account of its design and the light load of the front axle through the weight distribution and the short overhang of the chassis. When the turning circle was measured it was found to be 61ft for the left lock and 59ft for the right lock. The clutch and brakes, too, were light in their operation, making the driving of the Hillmaster a pleasant task.

vehicle, seemed adequate for the job. The handbrake was tested at a speed of 20mph and showed a Tapley meter reading of 31%.

Altogether the Rowe Hillmaster is the class of vehicle that will appeal not only to the operator but to the passenger as well, for its riding comfort is of a high standard, achieved mainly by excellent suspension, which is controlled by Telaflo shock absorbers on the front springs — these are effective on the rebound only — and long semi-elliptic springs. The engine too is conducive to comfort in view of its quietness and smoothness and the only murmur I could detect from it at any time was a slight periodic noise at 30mph in fourth gear. The Whitson body with which the chassis is equipped provides much comfort for the passenger in its luxury seating and good visibility.

Update

The Rowe Hillmaster was another design which, although receiving praise from the trade press, failed

Above: **Although not an exhibit at the 1954 Commercial Motor Show at Earls Court, there was a Rowe Hillmaster on display opposite the show's Demonstration Park.**

to make a significant impact in the market place. A total of five of the underfloor model were built between 1954 and 1958, when production ceased. One of the type survived into preservation.

Right: **The Rowe Hillmaster coach, fitted with Whitson 37-seat body, appeared in the 1955 Clacton Coach Rally.**

Above: **The Rowe Hillmaster was road tested for** *Passenger Transport* **in mid-1955 and it is seen here during the test.**

Although the underfloor engine had no need for it, a radiator grille was provided at the front end for appearance's sake.

Details in Brief of the Rowe Hillmaster

Engine: Meadows 4HDC horizontal four-cylinder engine. Develops 85bhp at 2,200rpm. Maximum torque, 230lb/ft at 1,350rpm. Bore, 120mm. Stroke, 120mm. Capacity, 5.43litre. Compression ratio, 16 to 1. Wet-type liners easily removed and replaced

Transmission: 14in diameter Borg & Beck single dry-plate clutch with ball bearing type thrust. Meadows five-speed overdrive top gearbox. Ratios: fifth, 0.76 to 1; fourth, direct; third, 1.75 to 1; second, 3.72 to 1; first, 6.12 to 1; reverse, 4.65 to 1

Rear Axle: Bevel gear axle fitted in a sturdy casing. Pinion, differential and hubs fitted with taper roller bearings with a standard ratio of 6.166 to 1. Wheel track, 66.875in

Front Axle: Of a robust design with sturdy king-pins and roller bearing thrusts. Wheel tracks, 72.25in

Steering: Fitted with Marles cam and double roller steering box, ratio 24.1. Full forward control

Brakes: Girling hydraulic brakes on all four wheels, assisted by a Clayton Dewandre servo unit. Rear brakes, 15in x 4.25in or 15in x 5in. Front brakes, 16in x 3in

Frame and Springs: Side-members of a high-grade steel have a section of 8.4375in x 0.219in strengthened by plates the length of wheelbase. Fitted with springs, (rear) 54in x 3in (front) 42in x 2.5in

Wheels and Tyres: Eight-stud steel wheels fitted with 8.25 x 20 tyres (twin rear)

Radiator: Strongly built with Clayton Dewandre tubes. Compact instrument panels

14 March 1956
——Bedford/Duple Super Vega——

With the redesigned bus and coach chassis, Bedford Motors have provided a vehicle which will be more popular than ever with the operator. Increasing the wheelbase to 18ft — 10in more than the previous model — has had the effect of allowing the overall length of the complete vehicle to be extended to the full 30ft, thus enabling the seating capacity of a typical coach body to be raised from 36 to 41 seats. As it is powered by the same engine units, either petrol or diesel, the latest model has a much greater earning capacity, appropriate to modern operating conditions, yet retains its established economy.

Whilst most of the features of the big Bedford passenger chassis are retained in the new model, the chassis frame has been modified with a flat top running from behind the cab position to the rear end. As the height of the frame from the ground is 2.625in more than on the previous model, it has eliminated the need for a step-up over the rear axle. These features have simplified the work of the coachbuilder who, as the chassis frame ends behind the rear spring hangers, can now design his bodywork so that the rear overhang is self-supported without the need to tamper with the frame extension. As there is a reduction in the overhang behind the rear axle from 7ft 1.75in to 3ft 9in, there is also some saving in chassis weight.

Petrol and Diesel Engines

The alternative power units for the Bedford chassis consist of a petrol engine developing 114.6bhp at 3,200rpm and a Perkins diesel engine which develops 108bhp at 2,700rpm. As a petrol unit the big Bedford engine has a fine record with operators for its long and trouble-free life, and is too well-known to require a full description. Of the six-cylinder overhead valve push rod type, it is mounted as a single unit with the gearbox on three rubber-insulated supports. It has push fit cylinder liners, a seven-bearing crankshaft, aluminium alloy pistons and chromium-plated top piston rings. Because of its smoothness and quiet running, this engine is particularly favoured by luxury coach operators and was of the type fitted to the coach which I tested recently.

Below: Elevation and side views of the Bedford SBG chassis. These show the redesigned flat-topped frame and reduced overhang. These have simplified the work of the coachbuilder and effected a reduction in chassis weight.

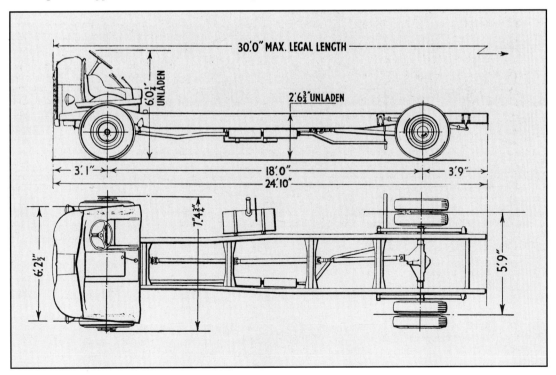

Left: The Bedford/Duple Super Vega looks slightly out of place amidst the suburban semi-detached houses during the *Passenger Transport* road test.

The power is transmitted through a 12in single dry plate clutch and a four-speed synchromesh gearbox, both of which are mounted as a unit with the engine. There are three open propeller shafts taking the drive to the back axle, with four Hardy Spicer needle roller bearing universal joints and two intermediate bearings. The fully floating rear axle has a hypoid final drive which is notably robust and quiet; there are alternative axle ratios of 6.821 and 5.833, the latter being fitted in the case of the vehicle which I was testing. An Eaton two-speed axle can also be fitted as an optional extra.

Extensive Equipment

The 8ft-wide 41-seat Duple Super Vega luxury body with which my test vehicle was equipped contained all the accessories that the modern coach operator could wish for. Whilst many of these are optional items and can be fitted only at extra cost, such is the price of the complete vehicle — only in the region of £3,200 — that when fully equipped, passenger comfort is greatly enhanced and the operator's pocket not too seriously affected. Lightweight composite construction is used for the body, consisting of steel lined pillars and steel or alloy reinforcing of all the stressed points.

It was a very cold day for the test, with temperatures well below freezing point. As it had been driven from the works at Luton to London to meet me, I was glad of the welcome warmth which had developed inside it from the three Clayton floor heaters. Wherever I sat in the coach the heat from them seemed to be about me, and I felt that at last the torture of cold travel had been overcome. With 41 seats on a chassis with a front-mounted vertical engine, one might think that seating would be cramped. This is certainly not so in the Super Vega, where I found that the leg room was sufficient and comfortable for the average person. The well-designed

seats are of Duple lightweight manufacture, having foam rubber cushions and squabs and trimmed with moquette and polyvinyl chloride plastic relief — but I still wonder why we must continue the use of headrolls which not only spoil the forward view for passengers but appear to be so infrequently used.

There is light in plenty inside the latest Duple Super Vega body, for besides the two large shaped Perspex panels in the canopy there are new rear dome corner windows and three roof lights, two of which are double opening units and one fixed. Supplied by Weathershield, the latter units have become the universal answer for letting in the light and sunshine from above. It is strange how such a unit as this, which was founded many years before the war, has only just found real favour with manufacturer and operator.

A Well-Laden Vehicle

Having received reports that snow conditions were less in the northwest part of London, I drove the coach in the direction of Watford Way. There was the usual test load of sandbags and five people aboard, which made up a gross weight of 7ton 11cwt 3qtr. As the unladen weight of this particular model is about 4ton 17cwt and the manufacturer's gross vehicle weight is 8ton 0.75cwt, we were well within the vehicle's load capacity.

Good Fuel Consumption

With its high back axle ratio of 5.833 to 1, this is essentially an express vehicle, so that I decided to carry out my fuel consumption test along the A41 in the direction of Aylesbury. Using the main tank, I filled up with Esso mixture and proceeded at a normal service speed in the region of 30mph and, in fact, I never exceeded 35mph. After covering a distance of 28 miles I found that we were on the outskirts of Aylesbury and my average speed had been just under 28mph. This returned a fuel consumption of 11.7mpg, which, considering the overload being carried and the very cold conditions not conducive to efficient engine running, seemed very good.

The main impressions gained during the first section of the road test were that the longer wheelbase of the coach had improved both its riding

comfort and stability, and that the increased weight made little difference to the engine performance. Visibility for the driver, and also for the passengers, is as good as one could desire in a vehicle with the engine mounted in this position. The double curved windscreens have a low line which gives a very close eye-to-ground view forward, while the curved quarter glasses and thin front pillars and screen frames make a notable contribution to the absence of blind spots. So good is the present driving position that the coach can be manoeuvred through tight traffic and narrow streets with ease and safety. Plenty of snow and a large expanse of glass made demisting a very important feature, but I found that even with it in operation it was still necessary to wipe the screen at regular intervals.

A 1 in 7 Climb

From Aylesbury I turned towards the Chiltern Hills in the direction of Ivinghoe, where nearby exists the steepest gradient in the locality, namely Bison Hill, with a maximum rise of 1 in 7. On this occasion I felt that the heavy load of the coach might have a detrimental effect on its hill-climbing ability, but the use of second gear at a speed of only 10mph for a short distance over the steepest part of the hill — and snow had fallen heavily just before we arrived — convinced me that it could tackle the severest of Continental mountain passes. Among these more tortuous roads the steering, too, proved light and positive, and it is worth noting that the turning circle of 64ft 6in has been unaffected by the increased wheelbase.

After passing through Whipsnade, I joined the A5 where I was able to do some fast driving, with all my passengers keeping an ever-open eye for the 'law'. Heavy traffic moves at a rapid pace on these main roads today and unless one does a certain amount of overtaking a low average speed must be expected. However, a lively Bedford engine and a useful third gear ratio, which can be engaged so smartly with the synchromesh mechanism, enabled me to keep the coach cruising at a speed of between 30 and 40mph for most of the way back to the Watford Way at Apex Corner. The maximum speed which I obtained on a level section of road was 53mph, a speed which I am sure even some of our faster coach drivers would not deride.

One expects quietness from a petrol engine, but the Bedford is certainly outstanding in this respect, and even when it is working at somewhere near the maximum revolutions it has the smoothness and quietness akin to a modern car. It must be remembered that the engine is alongside the driver and the cowling has no special soundproofing material.

Having driven the vehicle for some 50 miles, I had ample opportunity to test the efficiency of the footbrake. This might apply especially to the A5, where the hazards of a main road make one anxious to have the security of an efficient brake. Once, when I was compelled to make an emergency stop on a slippery road, I was thankful to find that the brakes reacted well and the vehicle pulled up in a dead straight line, despite the fact that there was a four-wheel lock.

Subsequent tests proved that from an average of two runs in opposite directions on a level road the footbrake had an efficiency of 68% (Tapley meter) from an emergency stop at 30mph, and 64% from 20mph. This gave stopping distances of 44ft 3in and 47ft 2in respectively. The handbrake had the high figure of 40%, which is about the best figure I have ever obtained from this particular brake. These figures were the result of several tests, as we had difficulty, due to road conditions, in avoiding wheel locking and sliding.

Acceleration figures were taken over the same section of road, and I found that through all four gears from rest to 20mph the time taken was 10.5sec, while 30mph was reached in 20.5sec. Such figures were only possible with the quick action of the gearbox, which has synchromesh engagement for second, third and top ratios. The excellent torque characteristics of this engine were well exhibited by the figures which I obtained when accelerating in top gear only from 10mph to 20mph and 10 to 30mph, the time taken being 13sec and 28.5sec respectively. The maximum torque of the engine is 236lb/ft at 1,400rpm.

Update
The Bedford SB chassis was introduced in 1950 as the basis for a 33-seater forward-control model. The petrol-engined version described in this test was classified SBG, although there was also a diesel-engined option (the SBO). Production of the SB model, with various modifications, continued for more than 20 years, with almost 50,000 constructed. A later reclassification, the NJM, continued in production until 1986, when Bedford ceased production.

Left: **Forty years ago it was possible to drive along roads like this without facing the ever-increasing problem of parked cars. The road is almost empty during the *Passenger Transport* test — and this was not only a consequence of the weather conditions.**

Details in Brief of the Bedford Passenger Chassis (Petrol Engine)

Petrol Engine: Bedford vertical six-cylinder engine. Bore and stroke, 3.875in x 4.25in. Capacity, 4.9litre developing 114.6bhp at 3,200rpm. Max torque, 236lb/ft at 1,400 rpm. Compression ratio, 6.3 to 1

Fuel Equipment: Six-phase downdraught Zenith 42 VIR-3 carburettor, with accelerator pump and part throttle economy valve. Oil bath air cleaner

Engine Cooling: Pressurised system. Circulation by Centrifugal pump. Thermostatic control

Transmission: Single dry-plate 12in clutch. Spring loaded centre and area of 133sq in. Gearbox, four-speed and reverse, synchromesh 2nd, 3rd and top. Ratios: 7.059 to 1, 3.332 to 1, 1.711 to 1, direct; reverse, 7.059 to 1. Three open propeller shafts in line with four Hardy-Spicer needle roller bearing universal joints

Rear Axle: Fully floating axle shafts. Hypoid final drive. Axle ratio, 5.833 to 1. Eaton two-speed axle is available as an optional extra

Steering: Semi-irreversible worm and sector type rigidly mounted on chassis frame side-member. Steering column connected to worm shaft by fabric universal; joint. Steering box ratio, 26 to 1

Brakes: Hydraulic brakes on all wheels with vacuum-servo assistance. Horizontal pull-up handbrake operates on rear wheels by cable. Total brake lining area, 498.4sq in

Frame and Springs: Deep channel section side-members of pressed steel, tapered to front and rear, with riveted cross-members. Side-members upswept over front axle and are flat topped from driver's bulkhead to rear end. Semi-elliptical laminated leaf springs front and rear, double-acting hydraulic shock absorbers front and rear

Wheels and Tyres: Pressed steel disc wheels with wide base rims, 6.00 to 20 wheels, offset 5.1in. 8.25-20 10-ply tyres

Electrical System: 12V lighting and stating. 500 Watt generator. Two 6V batteries in series. 129 Amp/hr at 20hr rate.

Beadle Canterbury Coach

Reduced passenger traffic in many areas and the need for a replacement unit for the large number of vehicles accommodating about 30 passengers introduced immediately after the war has led to the recent development of new models of this size. With a view to attracting potential buyers and obtaining a foretaste of the market for the smaller class, several were demonstrated this year at the Commercial Motor Show at Earls Court. Among them were the latest Beadle offerings — the Canterbury 29-seat coach and the Thanet 32-seat bus.

Both these models are based on a modified version of the Karrier Gamecock chassis which for public service use has been extended to provide a wheelbase of 14ft 9in instead of 11ft 9in. To provide improved riding qualities the rear springs have been made softer, while the public safety is cared for by the use of larger diameter and wider brake shoes on all wheels. The engine so far employed is the standard Rootes overhead valve inclined petrol engine, which is derated from 111bhp to 85bhp by governing the speed to 2,600rpm with a vacuum governor fitted to the Solex down-draught carburettor. The popular Rootes three-cylinder two-stroke diesel engine, however, is now available for use in this model.

The model made available for me to test by John C. Beadle (Coachbuilders) Ltd, of Dartford, was the Canterbury; this is a full-fronted luxury coach with a side entrance accommodated behind the nearside front wheel. Due to the position of the inclined engine over the front axle it is impossible to have a seat at the front alongside the driver, and this space is used for a railed-in luggage carrier. To eliminate the rear wheel-arch projection, the seats at the rear are mounted on a raised platform.

Metal construction is employed for the bodywork, the frame being of standard Metal Sections components with light timber packing where necessary to fix the exterior aluminium panels. The body is mounted on the chassis by body bearers which are bolted to steel angle brackets attached to the chassis side-members. All the bearers are insulated from the chassis frame with Balata packing. The front end is supported by Metalastik mountings and the rear end is secured by means of a steel truss panel forming the forward end of the rear luggage boot. The roof forming consists of timber roofsticks and longitudinals, the roofsticks being reinforced by steel carlines. An external door is fitted and an emergency hinged door is situated at the rear offside of the body.

Permanent ventilation is arranged at the front end and controlled by 'hit and miss' grids, while there are three roof extractors mounted along the centre line of the roof. In each side there are five double sliding windows; the main fixed windows have double-lip channel rubber glazing in the body framework. The remaining quarter and cab lights are glazed with Caltonrite rubber section.

The test coach was laden with sandbags and, including the driver, four passengers and test equipment, weighed 7ton 1cwt 2qtr, with axle loadings on the front of 2ton 15cwt and rear of 4ton 6cwt 2qtr. Unladen, the Canterbury weighs 4ton 6cwt, so that our vehicle was well overloaded. The speedometer registered 1,115 miles, most of this distance having been completed on demonstration runs at Earls Court.

Leaving the Dartford works of Beadle's, I drove in the direction of Farningham, intending to follow a route which would include Wrotham Hill, Maidstone,

Right: This was the John C. Beadle (Coachbuilders) Ltd stand at the 1956 Commercial Motor Show at Earls Court. On display were examples of the single-deck bus and coach models fitted with Rootes-built engines. The Canterbury coach on the left was destined for Timpsons and the 32-seat Thanet bus for Yorkshire Traction.

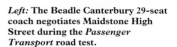

Canterbury are placed well back from the front of the body, but due to a deep windscreen and thin frame and front pillars, the forward and side vision remained good. The driver's seat is a comfortable semi-bucket pattern with two-way adjustment, and it is possible to give hand signals through the sliding window on the offside.

Along the Maidstone road from Farningham the Canterbury cruised comfortably at speeds between 40 and 45mph — later I found that it had a maximum speed in the region of 55mph — and it certainly rode well at speed with a negligible amount of pitching at the front.

All the mechanical parts used in the chassis are well-tried Karrier units which have established a reputation for reliable, silent and economical operation. Combined with the Beadle body, which has been designed with a view to reducing noise and vibration, it was not surprising that I found the coach travelled as quietly and smoothly at speed as when passing more slowly through built-up areas. In fact the engine was indiscernible when idling.

After proceeding through the busy streets of Maidstone, I turned from the main Ashford road to Hollingbourne to make an ascent of the long hill on the north side of the village; this is about a mile long and has a maximum gradient of 1 in 7. Although I approached the hill at 25mph in top gear, it soon became necessary to adopt the intermediate gears — an easy task with the synchromesh gearbox — and first gear for the final ascent. The time taken to complete this climb was 3min 25sec, and there was a temperature rise of the engine coolant from 192° Fahrenheit to 202°. Reversing to the steepest section of the hill, where the handbrake held the vehicle without pulling on that extra 'notch', I was able to make a smooth restart in first gear.

Charing and Canterbury, returning by way of the Medway towns. Weather conditions were fine and dry with an ambient temperature of about 45° Fahrenheit. An overall fuel consumption test was being made, for which the 16gal main tank had been filled with commercial petrol.

The narrow and tortuous road between Dartford and Farningham provided us with early proof of the manoeuvrability and liveliness of the Canterbury. The steering was light and positive, but lacked the amount of castor effect which I personally like. Naturally, being a petrol engine, it had that quietness and smoothness so desirable in the running of a luxury coach.

I have always been impressed with the efficiency of the synchromesh gearboxes manufactured by the Rootes Group and the unit fitted to this chassis was no exception, for gear engagement is both quick and positive. The gear lever, too, is well placed on the left-hand side of the driver. Unlike the larger Rochester coach, the driving position and steering on the

Acceleration and braking tests were made on a level stretch of the Ashford road which had a concrete surface. Using all gears from first to top, and taking the average figure of two runs, 20mph was reached in 13sec and 30mph in 21.5sec, while from 10mph to 30mph in top gear only, the acceleration time was 20.5sec to 20mph and 30sec to 30mph. Both sets of figures reveal the lively performance of the engine and indicate that whilst a higher back axle ratio might be fitted without adversely affecting the vehicle performance, there might be some improvement on fuel consumption.

The Girling servo-assisted hydraulic brake system employed on the Canterbury proved to be most effective. From both 20 and 30mph the Tapley meter recorded an efficiency of 83% — respective stopping distances of 16ft and 36ft, or 27ft per sec per sec. The handbrake, too, was above average, for from 20mph the efficiency was 39%, a stopping distance of 36ft. The lever for the latter follows normal goods vehicle practice by being on the left side of the driver.

Charing Hill was the next gradient where a low ratio was required. This time, however, second gear was sufficient to enable the top to be reached with a throttle that was only partly open. On reaching Canterbury the turning circle was measured, being 59ft 6in on both locks.

Returning along the A2 through Sittingbourne and Chatham, traffic increased to the disadvantage of our average speed. On reaching the Beadle works, our mileage for the complete test was 117 and the average running speed, excluding stops for refreshment, was about 28mph. A fuel consumption of 11.1mpg was returned, which I considered most satisfactory for this class of petrol-engined vehicle.

The standard of passenger comfort is high, and in particular I liked the composite seats with individual cushions, despite their high backs and unnecessary headrests which do much to obscure passengers' view. There is plenty of leg room, and during a short spell in the back seat I was impressed by the comfort and smoothness provided in a position which is frequently unpopular with certain passengers.

Above: The interior of the 29-seat Canterbury coach. From a modern perspective the seating looks cramped and the headroom less than generous, although the road test at the time praised the internal layout.

Below: Elevation and plan drawing of the Beadle Canterbury 29-seat coach which utilises a modified Karrier Gamecock chassis.

The price of the petrol-engine version of the Canterbury is £2,965; with a Rootes diesel engine it is £3,300. With the latter unit, the coach should appeal to the rural operator as a dual-purpose vehicle for either stage, excursion or private hire work. Wide luggage racks and a 75cu ft rear boot provide ample space for luggage and parcels.

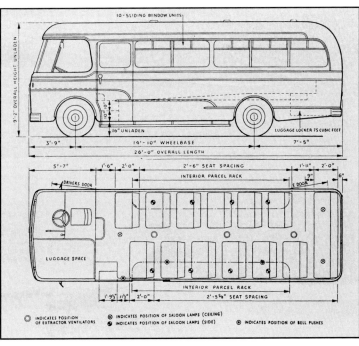

Update

John C. Beadle (Coachbuilders) Ltd of Thanet developed its integral buses and coaches in the immediate postwar years utilising components from other manufacturers' vehicles. It launched an underfloor, horizontal model at the 1948 Commercial Motor Show. A further development came in 1954 with the launch of a new model based upon the Commer. The smaller Canterbury (coach) and

Above: **The Canterbury coach caught in Maidstone bus station during the road test.**

Thanet (service bus) models followed, being based upon the Karrier Bantam chassis. Small numbers were produced before Beadle ceased manufacture in the late 1950s.

Brief Details of the Beadle Canterbury 29-Seat Coach

Petrol Engine:	Rootes ohv six-cylinder petrol engine developing 85bhp at 2,600rpm; maximum torque 216lb/ft at 1,200rpm. Engine positioned at the front end under floor	*Frame and Springs:*	High duty steel channel section 8in-deep frame with seven cross-members. Front springs 48in long and 2.75in wide, rear springs 46in long and 2.5in wide
Transmission:	Single dry plate, 11in clutch; four-speed synchromesh remotely controlled gearbox. Ratios are: fourth, direct; third, 1.838 to 1; second, 3.478 to 1; first, 7.227 to 1; reverse, 8.431 to 1	*Electrical Equipment:*	12V dynamo and Lucas starter, 121amp hr lead acid batteries, electric horn, side, tail and head lamps, with foot-operated dip switch
Rear Axle:	Spiral bevel, standard ratio 5.43 to 1	*Bodywork:*	All-steel frame construction and truss panels with resin-bonded plywood flooring. Full luxury composite seats with foam rubber cushions, squabs and headrest fillings. Trimmed in moquette and Vynide. Ten double sliding windows in polished alloy frames. Rear locker capacity 75cu ft with flap access. Clayton demister and flashing trafficators
Front Axle:	Heavy high tensile I section steel forging, large diameter inclined king-pins		
Steering:	Cam and double roller steering unit — ratio 24.7 to 1. Steering wheel 18in diameter		
Brakes:	Hydraulic servo-assisted brakes, 16in diameter by 3in wide front, 15.25in x 4.25in wide rear. Total area, 437.5sq in	*Dimensions:*	Wheelbase: 14ft 9in Length: 26ft Width: 7ft 6in Weight: 4ton 8cwt

Just as running costs continue to rise, so do the prices of new public service vehicles, and it is small wonder that operators for some time have been anxious to obtain a single-decker of maximum dimensions built to a simple design which is economical to operate and cheaper to purchase. The new Albion Aberdonian, known as the type MR11, certainly measures up to these requirements having been produced particularly with the interurban bus service in mind; however, it is also available as a coach chassis or for export.

The new chassis is largely the outcome of the good results which Albion Motors have achieved with their small Nimbus model. By using the resources of the Leyland Group, of which Albion is a member, it has been possible to employ the Leyland Comet O350 engine and several other standard units, resulting in a robust and economical machine. The chassis weighs about 17cwt less than the Leyland Tiger Cub and is suitable for 30ft by 8ft single-deck bodywork at a gross weight including load of 8.5ton. The price, it is understood, will be under £2,000 and some £450 less than that of the Tiger Cub.

Demand for Cheaper Vehicles

The demand for this class of vehicle is already proved from the fact that orders for about 100 have been received. Several well-known coachbuilders have bodywork of a light design to satisfy the Aberdonian's weight limit, while others have designs in preparation. Among the operators who have these vehicles in service or on order are the North Western, East Yorkshire, Northern General, PMT, Smith's of Wigan and Western SMT concerns. The last-named of these companies has a number of this model, one of which is employed on the London-Glasgow night express run. It was a similar vehicle we tested at the Albion works recently, which provided some excellent results.

As already mentioned, the Aberdonian resembles in its layout the Nimbus, but employs, in place of the

Below: **According to the test report hills of up to a gradient of 1 in 4 can be climbed in first gear with the Aberdonian. The test vehicle is seen below starting a comfortable climb in second gear up the 1 in 8 gradient at Blanefield with the Campsie Fells in the background.**

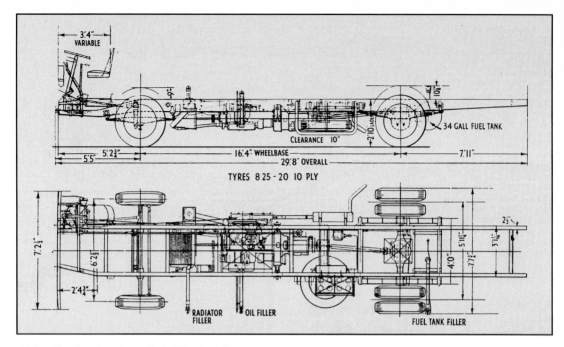

3'.4" VARIABLE

34 GALL FUEL TANK

CLEARANCE 10"

5'.5"   5'.2¾"

16'.4" WHEELBASE

29'.8" OVERALL

7'.11"

TYRES 8.25 - 20 10 PLY

7'.2½"

6'.2½"

2'.4¼"

RADIATOR FILLER   OIL FILLER

FUEL TANK FILLER

Albion diesel engine, the well-tried Leyland O350 horizontal diesel engine — the power unit for the Tiger Cub. For its new role this 5.76litre engine is governed to 2,000rpm to produce 94bhp; it has a maximum torque of 255lb/ft at 1,400rpm. The only other departure from standard is, following Albion practice, the introduction of a Glacier centrifugal lubricating oil filter, which is fitted at the base of the filler tube.

The drive is transmitted through a 13in diameter single dry-plate clutch which is hydraulically operated and an Albion five-speed gearbox with constant mesh and dog engagement on all ratios. To reduce the transfer of vibration from the engine to the chassis, the engine, clutch and gearbox are mounted as a unit by a flexible link mounting, which constrains the unit to oscillate on an axis between its centre of gravity and the propeller shaft front joint. At the rear of the gearbox there is a Holmes Holset type of torsion damper. The final drive is taken through a single tubular propeller shaft with the latest Hardy Spicer all-metal universal joint 1510 type to an overhead worm drive axle of the fully floating type with 7in centres. The differential assembly can be withdrawn from the one-piece forged axle case without removing the road wheels.

There is a conventional front axle in which the pivot pins are carried in plain brushes, the thrust being taken on shrouded bronze and steel bearings. This arrangement is such as to give a free-running bearing which has contributed largely to easy steering. The steering gear is of the Marles cam and double-roller type and the steering column is arranged so that the ball pin and the steering arm is in front of the axle, and the steering connecting rod runs back to the ball pin and the stub arm.

Simple Brake Layout

Similar suspension to the Nimbus is employed with semi-elliptic laminated springs, 51in long and 2.5in wide at the front and 60in long and 3.5in wide at the rear; Newton & Bennett double-acting telescopic shock absorbers are used at the front end only. The Clayton Dewandre servo system has enabled a simple vacuum hydraulic brake layout to be installed; the brakes have Girling two-leadingshoes. With brake drums of 16in by 2.5in at the front and 15.25in by 5in at the rear, there is a total footbrake area of 451sq in or 53sq in/ton for the maximum gross weight of 8.5ton.

The frame of the Aberdonian is parallel, being of pressed steel channel section braced with tubular and pressed steel cross-members bolted in position. The maximum section of the side-members is 8.375in deep, 0.25in thick, with 2.5in flanges. At the front overhang — which is 5ft 5in — the frame is downswept to a level 7.75in below the remainder of the frame; this is to allow a low floor height at the entrance. A rear frame drop extension can be supplied if required for luxury coach luggage boots.

Other equipment includes a cylindrical 34gal fuel tank — giving a range of over 500 miles — which is suspended transversely between the frame members behind the rear axle, and an AC oil bath air filter mounted on the offside of the frame in front of the engine. There is CAV 24V lighting and starting equipment with the 121 amp/hr batteries carried externally on the nearside frame in front of the rear axle. The 8.25 by 20 10-ply tyres are standard equipment all round.

The Aberdonian which I tested had been fitted with a 39-seat coach body built by Walter Alexander

Left: Elevation and plan diagrams of the Albion Aberdonian chassis which was designed for economical bus and coach operation. It was suitable for lightweight bodies of 30ft x 8ft dimensions and had a gross overall weight of 8ton 10cwt.

Right: Stirling was the furthest point reached during the road test of the Albion Aberdonian. Here the test vehicle, Western SMT No KI1384, is pictured at Stirling with the castle forming a dramatic backdrop.

Below right: PMT No SN8745, a Weymann-bodied Albion Aberdonian, is pictured in the Ironmarket, Newcastle-under-Lyme, in 1971. This was one of 34 44-seat buses put into service during 1958. *A. Moyes*

& Co (Coachbuilders) Ltd of Stirling. This Scottish firm is renowned for its lightweight design which, although lacking nothing in comfort and luxury, enables an unladen vehicle weight of only 5ton 5.25cwt to be obtained. The vehicle had been loaded with weights arranged beneath the seats and in the rear luggage boot. Its gross weight was 8ton 8cwt, so that, with two persons acting as driver and observer, the overall weight was just over the limit of 8ton 11cwt; front and rear axle loadings were about 3ton 4cwt and 5ton 6cwt.

Scottish Road Test

The route followed from the Albion works at Scotstoun, near Glasgow, was through the

northwest outskirts of Glasgow by way of Strathblane and Buchlyvie to Stirling; the return route was through Drymen. Although the roads used are of A category with very good surfaces, they are narrow and in places very undulating, but are regularly used by the stage services of W. Alexander & Sons Ltd, and the coach tours of many English and Scottish operators. Being supplied to Western SMT for express services, the coach tested was fitted with the higher of the two axle ratios available, which was 5.2 to 1. This, however, did not adversely affect the performance over the hilly sections of the route

through the Campsie Fells; on the contrary I was most impressed by its top gear behaviour. It seemed that this particular axle ratio would be suitable for most purposes. In fact, operators may soon have the opportunity of a higher ratio if the new Albion six-speed gearbox, including overdrive, which was introduced recently as a replacement for the standard five-speed unit, is made available in the Aberdonian.

Easy handling is a marked feature of the Aberdonian for not only is the directional control of the steering good but it has an effective castor action, while road shocks cannot be felt at the steering wheel.

Left: Six Albion Aberdonians were supplied to the North Western Road Car Co Ltd in mid-1957. They were fitted with 42-seat MCW bodies.

Below left: Pictured at Shoebury Market, Shoeburyness, Southend Corporation No 202 was an Albion Aberdonian fitted with a Weymann 45-seat body. *G. R. Mills*

direction. From rest, through the gears from second to top, 20mph was reached in 11.5sec and 30mph in 24.5sec. The excellent torque characteristics were demonstrated when accelerating in top gear from a speed of about 10mph to 20 and 30mph, which were reached in 20.25sec and 38sec respectively.

Efficient Brakes

Through the test I had found the brakes most effective, providing a great sense of security. Over the same stretch of road used for the acceleration tests, I tried the brakes against the Tapley meter. On the dry tarmac surface an emergency footbrake application at 20mph produced a figure of 61% efficiency and at a speed of 30mph, 58.5%. A handbrake application operating on the rear wheels only produced a 30% figure, which is good for a loaded vehicle. In each case the vehicle stopped smoothly, evenly and dead in line.

Later, I made a continuous brake application down a long descent of about 1.5 miles at Blanefield where the maximum gradient was approximately 1 in 8, and the vehicle kept to about 18mph. Immediately following this a full brake application was made at 20mph which showed a decrease of 14% efficiency on the earlier test on the level. However, on the steepest part of this hill the Aberdonian pulled away comfortably in second gear and there was certainly no doubt about the hill-holding capabilities of the handbrake.

The Aberdonian is a classic example of how a modern public sector vehicle can be designed to lighter standards without sacrificing too much of the necessary robust qualities required for this class of service. Its simple layout employing well-tried standard units arranged for easy maintenance will undoubtedly appeal to the operator, particularly on rural bus services with fluctuating traffic, and the small coach operator who has to rely on seasonal work that provides only a limited income. It is a worthy addition to the Leyland-Albion range of vehicles and should prove highly successful providing operators and coachbuilders keep it within the stipulated weight limit.

Update

The Albion Aberdonian was launched in 1957 and sold well in its native Scotland, but less well elsewhere. It was effectively a lightweight version of the Leyland Tiger Cub. Production of the Aberdonian ceased in 1961.

This is obviously the result of the design described earlier. Short movements of the lever make gear changing quick and positive. This is connected to the gearbox by a long tubular shaft with universal joints which make for smooth action.

20mpg Fuel Consumption

My first fuel consumption test took place from a point on the Aberfoyle road to Buchlyvie — a distance of seven miles. Over this undulating road I made approximately three 15sec stops to the mile at an average speed of 19mph. This resulted in a fuel consumption of 12mpg — a satisfactory return for normal stage carriage work. The second test consisted of a nonstop run from Stirling to Drymen, the coach remaining in top gear for the full distance of 20 miles. At an average speed of 35mph a consumption of 20.6mpg was obtained, and it appears that under normal long-distance operating conditions, a figure of 20-plus might be regularly obtained.

On a straight level stretch of road I had the Aberdonian running on the governor at a speed of 46mph. In these days when coach operators are demanding higher maximum speeds, this might appear to be insufficient. It is for coaching, therefore, that the six-speed gearbox with overdrive would certainly have an appeal. Acceleration and braking tests were conducted on the straight level road approaching Stirling. Figures for the former were obtained by an average of two runs, one in each

—— Seddon Rear-Engined Bus ——

Special attention to local needs has brought Seddon Diesel Vehicles Ltd, of Oldham, Lancashire, into the front rank of heavy commercial vehicle manufacturers; in fact, their bus and coach chassis are probably much better known abroad than at home, for large numbers of Seddon machines are now operating in the Far East, Africa and on the Continent. The company has recently obtained an order from Hong Kong for 100 Seddon bus chassis.

A few months ago a prototype rear-engined passenger chassis was produced for Bangkok and this vehicle has been operating successfully ever since on long-distance services in Siam (Thailand). More recently the Bermuda Transportation Board ordered through the Crown Agents for the Colonies three similar models but with a shorter wheelbase, to add to their already 100% Seddon fleet of 60 buses. Thus the Seddon Mark 18 chassis, as it is called, has become the only production rear-engined passenger vehicle in this country at the present time.

I was fortunate in being able to test one of the three buses destined for Bermuda, just before it was despatched to Birkenhead Docks for shipping. These vehicles seat 32 passengers and were completed throughout in the Seddon works, utilising an all-metal body of the firm's own design. They will have a dual role in Bermuda, being used either on the stage services which are operated around Hamilton or on luxury tours of the island, which cater mainly for American visitors. For the latter reason, in particular, the new vehicles have been given an 'Americanised' styling with sloping side windows. There is a manually operated jack-knife door at the front for one-man operation when in use as a stage carriage.

The chassis is notable for its straightforward layout with the vertical Perkins P6 diesel engine underslung between the main frame members at the rear. This engine, which develops 83bhp at 2,400rpm, has a world-wide popularity and is backed by a very fine service organisation. No special arrangements have been necessary for cooling the engine, the radiator being mounted directly behind at the extreme rear and has a large 22in diameter puller type fan which draws the air in the normal manner through the radiator.

The chassis dimensions meet all present British requirements and although the engine is mounted longitudinally within the frame with the gearbox as a unit it has a permissible rear overhang. The drive from the David Brown five-speed gearbox is taken through a 12in-long propeller shaft to the pedal-driven rear axle. With a wheelbase of 13ft 10in, the front overhang is 4ft 11.5in, and the rear is 7ft 11.125in.

The bodywork has been designed for interior coolness with special windows supplied by Northern Windscreens of Manchester. These have a lower half which can be raised in three portions, allowing the airstream to pass round the body of the passenger instead of the face; there are also waist-high ventilators at the front. The roof is double-skinned and padded with insulation, while the floor is of chequer plate aluminium. There are two Weathershield roof lights and the reclining seats have a central armrest; the latter were also manufactured in the Woodstock factory. The absence of luggage racks gives the whole vehicle an airy atmosphere which is so important for tropical operation.

Below: **The Seddon Mark 18 chassis. This particular example was one of the batch supplied to Siam (Thailand).**

Left: A detail shot showing the positioning of the rear engine fitted to the Seddon Mark 18 chassis.

Below: Elevation and plan diagrams of the Seddon Mark 18 rear-engined bus. According to *Passenger Transport* at the time, the chassis's general arrangement should appeal to overseas operators who require a vehicle which is easy to maintain. The power unit was the Perkins P6 diesel engine and the chassis was fitted with a David Brown five-speed gearbox with normal manual operation.

The test was undertaken in the undulating region around Oldham on a cool summer day with an ambient temperature of about 55° Fahrenheit. Unfortunately the vehicle was unladen, due to the fact that it had to go immediately from my test to the dock for loading. In this condition the unladen weight was 4ton 3cwt, with a rear axle loading of 2ton 18cwt. The first test was undertaken with driver and two passengers over a route from the works through Shaw to Middleton, Bury and Rochdale. The round trip was 28 miles and was covered at an average speed of 24mph, being mainly through an urban area; there was the usual number of stops for traffic and the resultant fuel consumption of 12.32mpg under these difficult conditions was most satisfactory.

Over the variety of road surfaces riding seemed particularly good and despite the unladen condition of the vehicle there was only a slight amount of pitching at the front. The rear engine cover is insulated against sound and heat, but the area behind the full-width rear seat is not covered in and one might have anticipated that engine noise would be pronounced. This was not the case, however, and it was only when sitting well to the rear of the vehicle that the engine was at all perceptible. In its present position the engine is most accessible, because the centre portion of the rear seat can be raised and the engine cowling easily removed, thereby making all parts of the engine most accessible.

Acceleration and braking tests were carried out on a level wide stretch of road at Hollinwood. Again making allowances for the absence of load the Seddon Mark 18 showed that it possessed excellent performance characteristics. Accelerating from rest through the gears from second to top, 20mph was reached in 11.5sec and 30mph in 24sec. In top gear the figures revealed the sterling qualities and high torque of the Perkins engine, when 20mph was reached in 15sec and 30 in 25sec. All these results were an average of two runs taken in opposite directions over the same stretch of road.

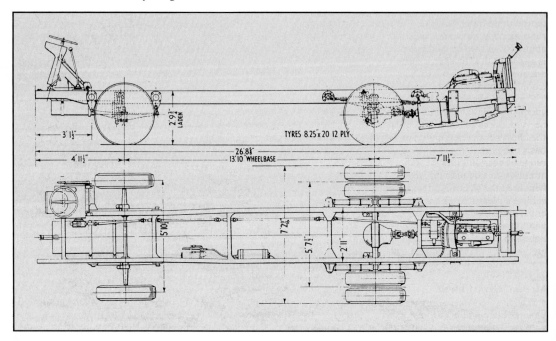

Right: A review view of one of the Seddon Mark 18 vehicles supplied to Siam in 1957. The caption at the time noted that the radiator will be larger on future models.

Below right: Looking slightly incongruous on the moors above the Seddon Works, this shot illustrates well the bodywork of the Seddon Mark 18s supplied to Siam.

Powerful Hydrovac Brakes

The brakes, which are power-assisted by a tandem Hydrovac servo system, proved most effective. An emergency application of the footbrake produced a Tapley meter reading of 74% at 20mph and 75% at 30mph. In each case the brakes worked progressively and there was an absence of wheel marks on the road; the vehicle stopped dead in line without any sign of pulling to the left or right. The handbrake figure at 20mph was 25%, which did not compare so favourably with the footbrake. Later, however, on a gradient of 1 in 6 it was found to hold the vehicle most satisfactorily.

Afterwards, I drove the bus on a circular run of about 20 miles across the Pennines through Denshaw and Delf (sic), where Buckston's Road in Shaw was climbed; this has a ruling gradient of about 1 in 12 with sections of up to 1 in 6. Over this road, which is about 1.5 miles long, the steepest gradient was climbed in second gear with the throttle only two-thirds open at a road speed of about 10mph. The temperature had been 132° Fahrenheit under normal running conditions and this had only increased by about 30° at the top of the ascent. From these tests it is apparent that cooling is quite adequate for the most extreme tropical conditions.

To distribute the weight more evenly the 33gal flat fuel tank has been mounted at the front between the chassis frame members; on the basis of our test this will give a range of over 400 miles. This attention to axle loading has benefited the steering, making the vehicle a pleasure to handle around either traffic-laden streets or winding country roads. It was both light and directionally positive with an absence of road shocks at the steering wheel.

Manual Gear Change

One problem which presents itself with a rear-engined vehicle is the gear selection. To simplify this, it has been the usual practice to use either a synchromesh or automatic gearbox. In the case of the Seddon, a normal constant mesh gearbox is employed which is operated by a centrally mounted remote gear lever connected through a universally jointed tube. Despite the length of the linkage I could change gear without difficulty, there being just sufficient engine noise to assist me. The clutch is hydraulically operated.

For the driver there is a Chapman's pedestal seat adjustable in two directions, and a glass fibre pedestal surrounding the steering column contains a full range of instruments. The all-round visibility from this position is good and all the controls are well to hand, including the door operating handle and the handbrake lever, which is on his left.

Left: The contemporary caption reads: 'The bodywork of the three vehicles for Bermuda was constructed throughout in the Seddon Works. To satisfy the tastes of the principal visitors to that island a pseudo-American appearance has been adopted. To assist ventilation, opening units have been fitted at the waist of the front bulkhead.'

Below left: At the conclusion of the *Passenger Transport* road test the bus returned to the Seddon Works at Oldham, Lancashire.

Seddon have certainly proved with their latest model that a rear engine arrangement does not necessitate complicated design, and as in the case of the Mark 18 can utilise standard components, avoiding unnecessarily high costs in a unique design. In fact its cost should be equivalent to a forward engine design, making it most competitive with foreign makes of rear engine vehicles. It also has the advantage of a simpler layout, which should appeal to operators overseas where maintenance is of a low standard.

It is understood that this chassis will be available with the Perkins R6 Series II diesel engine developing 102bhp for operators requiring a more powerful unit. This will necessitate a 13in diameter clutch and a David Brown 45/3 five-speed gearbox.

Update

During the period Seddon continued to more active in the export market. The Mark 18 was followed by the Mark 19 in 1959. Again this model was sold primarily overseas, although the prototype, fitted with an AEC horizontal engine and fitted with a Harrington body, was supplied to a UK operator (Thorne of Bubwith).

Details of Seddon Mk 18 Rear-Engined Bus			
Diesel Engine:	Perkins P6 vertical six-cylinder four-stroke engine with indirect injection. Develops 83bhp at 2,400rpm. Maximum torque, 203lb/ft. Bore, 3.5in. Stroke, 5in. Capacity, 288.6cu in. Engine mounted at the rear of the chassis between the frame members	*Brakes:*	Girling two leading shoe hydraulic system with Lockheed tandem Hydrovac vacuum servo assistance. Drum diameter, (front) 16in (rear) 15.25in. Lining width, (front) 3in (rear) 4.25in. Total brake area, 376.5sq in
Transmission:	Single dry plate 12in diameter clutch. David Brown 542 five-speed constant mesh gearbox. Ratios: fifth, direct; fourth, 1.47 to 1; third, 2.141 to 1; second, 3.75 to 1; first, 6.61 to 1; reverse, 6.28 to 1. Single short propeller shaft with Hardy Spicer needle roller bearing universal joints	*Frame and Springs:*	Pressed steel channel section with six bolted cross-members. Semi-elliptic springs with telescopic shock absorbers at front and rear. Front, 11 leaves, 43in centres and 3.25in wide. Rear, 15 leaves, 60in centres and 3in wide
		Electrical Equipment:	12V compensated control system with two 6V 116amp hr batteries
Rear Axle:	Fully floating spiral-bevel rear axle. Ratio 6.66 to 1	*Radiator:*	Mounted at extreme rear with 20in puller type fan for cooling
Steering:	Marles cam and double roller unit. Steering wheel 21in diameter		